Surviving the ~~Holidays~~ HELL-i-DAZE

By Miss Olivia Michele Giacomini

DEDICATION

This book is dedicated to those crazy individuals I love so much
and call my family.
(Fortunately, I am blessed to include many of my friends
in this "family" category).

Mom, Dad, Seana—thanks for the kooky childhood memories,
I wouldn't have them without you!

'Chelle & Sandy—thank you for being zany enough to support
& join me on our wacky adventures in life.

Dinah—thank you for your quick-witted sarcastic self & being
the best God Mother our dog could ever have.

Most of all, a huge thank you to those three nutty guys who
make my life so chaotic, insanely fun,
& absolutely wonderful.
Dave, Ryan & Eric, you are my everything
(and I don't just mean great material for my stories,
but it helps)!
Love you three to the moon & back, to infinity-squared.
(And back)!

PREFACE

As always, I am going to preface by saying that this book is loosely based on my adventures in everyday life. But for legal reasons, I am pointing out that it is fiction. If you think part of this book is about you, well, it's not—just purely coincidence. No real names of people, other than Dave's, are found in this book, other than in the dedication—because again, it's fiction. And YES, you may read my name in this book, but it's simply been lent as the name for the fictional character narrating the book. Got it? Good!

So as my legendary literary hero Erma Bombeck, once said, *"If you can't make it better, you can laugh at it."*

Now let's get on with the book, shall we?

~

Writer's Block

December 2013

I was driving home from work today and had a thought that if I could just write again for a living, I would be so happy. I say "again," because that's what I used to do for a living. Yes, it was decades ago, but still. I was a published writer and I made money doing what I love. So why did I stop? Simple. I didn't make ENOUGH money doing what I love—so I got real and moved on. But like a long lost lover, I will always hold a dear spot in my heart for writing. And right now, I am feeling the urge to rekindle that ole flame in a big way!

Maybe it's because it's Christmas. Maybe it's because I finally have a week off work with few obligations tearing me in five million different directions for the first time in years. Who cares why, the point is, I've decided to think about getting serious about putting pen to paper again. (Okay, we all know I mean keying on a laptop while I sip my favorite beverages). Regardless, it's time.

Of course, speaking of time, it took me an hour just to pick out a template for my new blog. I can't tell you how much I analyzed and agonized over just the perfect format in which to bestow my witticisms and other wise anecdotes. In the end, went with something basic (but knowing myself, as I do—that won't last long).

Now I'm just struggling to make up my mind on what to write about. Maybe I should write about the idiots out shopping on December 23rd? You know the ones—the honking maniacs behind wheels duking it out over who gets the closest parking spot.

I'd love to shout, "Save some time, moron and park a few more feet away. You would've been in the store AND in line by now! (Cuz there's nothing left anyway)!!!" Yeesh!

Hmmm...I could write about the appalling behavior inside the stores??? People are ripping ugly ass sweaters out of each other's hands, diving for the last ratty scarf and scouring the store for any scrap of resemblance to something that looks meaningful to give their beloveds.

I can't help thinking, "Good luck losers! Besides, nothing says 'I've been thinking of you' more than shopping at the last second!" (I say when you wait this long, you get what you get and you don't throw a fit).

Or dare I write about the worst of all those people? The parents, (if-you-will), who have the audacity to scream insults at poor, defenseless and exhausted retail clerks with rants of how the employees are the evil demons of hell and the sole reason why their child's Christmas has been ruined this year—because the (insert toy of choice here) is no longer available. I mean seriously?

That's when it takes everything I have not to interject, get right up in some of these idiot's faces and square off, "Please note, it is December 23rd you freak! If you really wanted that new rated-M warfare video game for your 4 year old, you should've ordered it weeks ago—or at least entered the purchasing game back on Black Friday. Really?"

(SIDENOTE: Geez, I look at it this way, by now, if I haven't gotten you anything, you ain't gettin' nothin' for Christmas! Unless, you make me feel guilty—and that, my friend, is what a good old fashioned checkbook is for)!

But alas, I probably won't spout these remarks, because if I'm brutally honest, I can never think of those things right then and there on the heat of the moment. Ya know? It's always when it's a few moments too late that I am ready to spew the insults of the century in rebuttal to asinine actions. I think it's a shock-mechanism. My brain is simply in such disbelief that someone could behave so appalling, that my mouth just can't sync with my brain on a phenomenal verbal retort. But I CAN write! I could write about all these great things I would have said, (and secretly wish I would bump into the person just one more time so I could literally read them MY riot act)!

But tonight, I'm just too excited about writing again to even think of anything to write about! Right?!

Miss O.M.G.

"Every time I make plans to eat better,
I hear my stomach laughing."
~Author Unknown

JANUARY

GRATITUDE & KINKY POSITIONING

For a New Year's Resolution, I resolved not only to be more healthy and fit (like most of the rest of the world), but to also be more grateful about my life. That said, I decided to do as the "experts" say and journal those cherished moments of thankfulness. So here goes:

JANUARY GRATITUDE JOURNAL:

January 1st-
Today I am grateful that my family is together, I have a clean house, and that none of my body parts fell off when I rediscovered yoga earlier this evening.

January 2nd-
Uh oh...live and learn...never do yoga on a full stomach. I fell asleep in the Child's Pose. Oops! (Thankful I didn't puke during Downward Dog).

January 3rd-
Pilates is a reminder of why so many people should always have sex with the lights OFF! Seriously. OH. MY. GAWD! As I dragged my ass to the gym tonight, I got to class just in time to find a spot near the front of the class—practically pressed against the studio's wall-length mirror.

It wasn't long before I found myself praying for a blindfold. Trying to squeeze my eyes shut wasn't working because some of those poses would make my eyelids pop right back open. I was trapped in a nightmare—forced to watch us all doing these contortions in said mirror. I knew I'd never be able to unsee what I had seen. And while this horror show agonizingly continued, I couldn't help but think, "GROSS!!!! I am never going to be seen naked again...and I'm never playing that "body twister" game with the giant dots either for the rest of my life!!!" (If anyone ever reads this journal entry, just saying, better to be lucky and laugh reading about it, than to lose your lunch seeing it in person)!!!

What? Seriously, I'm not being negative, I'm not body shaming—I'm just being honest. When you are upside down and contorted in weird positions, not too many people truly look fabulous. They look, well, er... AWFUL...myself, especially, included!!! (Yes, at first I was being self-critical and began the class with complete self-loathing of watching the rolls and lumps and bumps, I never knew I had, burst out through my exercise pants. (Thank goodness for Lycra)! But in the midst of feeling humiliated, I decided to check the room and see if anyone else looked as hideous as me. Guess what? Horrifyingly, they did! I think this was definitely a case of misery loves company. (And we all looked like the class couldn't end a second too soon)!

It was a train wreck, really. While I desperately wanted to stop watching, I found myself morbidly observing each and every grotesque move that my classmates and I engaged. PEOPLE! There are just some poses that one should NEVER be seen doing...EVER...not in public and not even private. It's just flat out WRONG!!! I think I am truly scarred for life!!!

Oh, almost forgot: gratitude. Um...ok, I am thankful I don't own a "body twister" game (although if I ever wanted to get back at my family for driving me crazy, I could force everyone to play—in leotards...hmmmm???). BLECH!

January 4th-

Why do the guys turn on the heater when I'm working out in our home gym (aka: playroom/guest room)? Good grief, don't they know it might make me actually perspire? Eewwww, GROSS!!! Don't get me wrong. I am all about working out daily. I even welcome a strenuous routine of exercise—as long as it doesn't make me sweat. I just don't do the wet stuff coming out of my pores.

It's like dogs. I love dogs! Love to pet them, snuggle with them, all that good stuff. But don't let them lick me. It's disgusting. I mean, have you seen where they've had that tongue? 'Cuz let me tell you, my dogs can put their tongues where I certainly cannot on my body, (and for the record, I'm perfectly okay with that). There is NOTHING that ruins a "welcome home" greeting more than to have your loving dog run up to you with its endearing wagging tail, just to lick your face after it just licked its ass. Just saying.

But you wanna know what's worse? I used to be an elementary school teacher for many, many years. I actually stopped teaching the itty bitties because of snot. Yup, it's true. I would have to constantly steady my gag reflex because the kids were constantly picking their noses and wiping on the carpet, or each other—and then they'd want to come hug me…(one moment please, while I run to the toilet to puke).

Ok, I'm back now—YUCK! So in summation, I just say no to sweat, saliva and snot. Enough said.

January 5th-
What am I thinking? Who can workout with fresh, oatmeal chocolate chip cookies just out of the oven and an icy glass of milk calling her name???

I am so thankful for those cookies. They not only taste delicious, but they are saving me time, because instead of working out today, I am eating those. (And I can certainly eat cookies faster than I can exercise—so they really are a godsend)!

Okay, now some may think this is a bad choice, but may I remind you that these are OATMEAL Chocolate Chip Cookies—so they are a healthy choice—don't believe me? Look up oatmeal on the internet. It's healthy I tell ya! I think I may even have some more for dinner, (boy are these cookies saving me a ton of time today, now I won't even have to cook)! And you know what else I just noticed? Every time I take a bite, my pedometer thinks I'm moving. So there you go. Healthy eating and exercise, all in one! Yay me! I think I just discovered a new diet. I should write a book about it, <u>That's the WEIGH the Cookie Crumbles</u>.

January 6th-
Miss OMG is interrupting her regularly scheduled exercise program to eat a HUGE piece of homemade, piping hot, ooey gooey apple pie...scrumptious! Wait. Something's wrong with this picture! Who stops in the middle of a workout to go eat pie, because she's hungry? ME! That's who! Plus, I decided after the great new diet book I was going to write, I should do some research on a sequel—and this pie has apples in it. Works for me!

January 7th-
Bizarre things happen in the Giacomini House when the tv satellite dish thingy goes out. I even saw my husband do something I haven't seen him do in about five years: he began exercising! What the heck?! I swear I almost fainted. Is that all it takes? Geez, one more day of this tv outage and he may even join a gym!!!

In his physical fitness defense, my dearest does play sports, he just does not like to exercise on a regular basis. (Yes, this is an official CYA statement to save my marriage).

While I am grateful my husband is working out, I did discover why my dearest darling was taking to huffing, puffing, stretching and such. It was simply to avoid an evening of actually having to talk to me. *shaking my head*

His avoidance of communication with yours truly is something that mystifies me. I don't get it. I'm fairly up on current events, kind of, (except for sports, which he loves—I just kinda don't care so much to remember all those teams and stats and stuff). I can carry on a conversation for hours and hours and hours. Further, I think our conversations spark great ideas—like new projects for us to do together. So I cannot understand why the moment I shared these feelings with him earlier today, he looked me straight in the eye and asked, "Do you know where my red sports bottle is? I'm going to go play basketball."

It was like he didn't even hear a word I said. Well, two can play at that game mister. So, while he was off playing hoops, I was off to find my own bottle—one that had some "red" in it!

What? Wine Drinking, it's a sport. (I even buy the bottles with the gold medals to prove it)!

January 8th-
It's a beautiful morning here at home today.
Sitting here staring out my bedroom window,
watching people outside running, this way and
that.

Reminds me I'm going to take up running today
too! Runnin' to Costco, runnin' to the grocery
store, runnin' to get my hair done, etc. Heck, who
has time to jog with all that runnin' around?

January 9th-
(Nine days in...I discovered I wasn't really writing
anything about gratitude. I hate dieting, and am
not a fan of exercise, if I'm brutally honest. So I
checked myself into the Fitness Protection
Program—but that's whole other story).

~

SHOULD I STAY OR SHOULD I GO?
I grew up in a family where my parents did not
make New Year's celebrating a top priority, at all.
If I'm totally honest, when I was a kid I sort of
thought my parents were kinda boring on New
Year's because of this mentality, or lack thereof.
It was nothing for them to traipse off to bed while
my sister and I stayed up 'til midnight to ring in
the new year together.

Looking back, I think the allure of NYE was the opportunity to have permission to be loud and annoying for about five minutes at midnight, (banging our pots and pans outside and whooping it up), more than the holiday itself. It was exciting to my sister and me. I mean in our family, five minutes of hell raising goes a long way—a complete year, to be exact!

It wasn't until I was a parent that I began to understand my parents' "Early to Bed" NYE philosophy. I get it—child raising is exhausting! Especially with our kids! (You need your well-deserved rest to be able to handle those munchkins the next day—cuz there are no days off in child rearing).

My husband and I were not those parents who did the 9pm PST NYE celebration to get our kids to go to bed early though. We were lucky and didn't have to. Honestly, our kids could care less about NYE. (Yup, probably got that from my side of the family). Every day they raised hell until they were exhausted and then they either crashed out wherever they were or flat out put themselves to bed. (In reflection, I guess our kids really are angels)! Who knew?

As our kids got older, I began to see the light. First of all, I began to understand why my parents didn't like going out to parties on NYE: too many drunk drivers. Right? It's crazy! You know, it just kind of hits you one day that you've got responsibilities. For us, that's our boys. We decided putting ourselves in that kind of danger is kinda like riding a roller coaster without buckling up—it's a wild time, but the chances of it ending well are not great.

Equally, I also have learned the hard way that I do not like hangovers. The older I get, the longer the hangovers hang OVER. So to survive, about 15 or so years ago I adopted the idea that your first day of the year will reflect how the rest of your year will be. Let me tell you, I now sing praises of joy when I wake up on New Year's Day with no hangover and actually able to remember the fun we had the night before! It really is a best kept secret.

So as an older and wiser celebrator I've learned to enjoy a variety of ways to celebrate. Some years we are super exhausted from work and it's hard to stay awake for the midnight festivities. (Although I've also discovered a fantastic tip: try falling asleep during a movie, then when you wake up, you'll be refreshed and ready to rock, roll and ring in the new year)!

If you really want to pull an all-nighter, be sure your "neighbors" set off fireworks for 40+ minutes at midnight in the surrounding neighborhoods; thus, freaking out your dog, making her cry & whine until you come downstairs to console her—for the REST. OF. THE. NIGHT.

Hmmm...since I now believe what you do for New Year's Day is an indicator for the rest of the year, it's a good thing I plan to have breakfast in bed, served by my hubby this next New Year's Day! (Gotta offset the night of canine madness, right)?

~

GOT MY RIGHT TO PARTY

Hindsight is hysterical. Now, when I look back at my "hellbent-to-party days," I actually remember the first year I knew my mindset was changing. Sick with pneumonia AND bronchitis, I was bound and determined to make it out to a NYE party at what we affectionately refer to as "The Zoo." This is the home (more specifically, the barn/out building), of my brother-from-another-mother & sister-from-another-mister—and a party there is NEVER to be missed.

I know what you are thinking, "Who the hell goes out sick as a dog like that?" I do! But don't judge me people, it was 1999, so I was "going to party like it was 1999." (You youngins probably won't catch that reference—ask your hip grandma what that meant back in the olden days, she'll school ya). Plus, we were ready to embrace the calamity that Y2K was about to unleash—and we wanted to do it together with all our friends—kinda like preparing for a Zombie Apocalypse. (SPOILER ALERT: The wrath never unfolded, 1/1/2000 came and went without a hitch, for the most part...and for those of you whippersnappers who haven't faintest clue what I'm referring to there either, Google it)!

Again, I'll never forget this party, because a dear friend walked up to us at 10pm to say her good-byes. I thought she was nuts, because the party was heating up to a nice rolling boil. But she confided that it was her romantic fantasy to ring in 2000 in a bubble bath with a glass of champagne.

We wished her well, and then I started to realize that bubble bath she referenced sounded pretty damn good—(plus, that steamy water would probably really loosen the mass of clinging phlegm in my lungs). So much to my husband's initial chagrin, (that is until he realized nudity was involved, when taking said bubble bath), we found ourselves heading off about 30 minutes later to do the same damn thing.

Funny thing is, I remember that bubble bath moment more than most other NYE celebrations. I had my fun with friends and I was going to wake up feeling no more worse than what my illness ailments were already causing. I'll never forget the candlelight and suds as we clinked our glasses at midnight. I mean come on—rub a dub, dub, having fun in the tub!!! Who forgets some good clean fun like that?

So with that memory from long ago lingering in our minds, this year we plan to ring in the New Year in the "neighborhood." Hey, I'm totally against drinking and driving, but I never said nuthin' about drinkin' and crawlin' home!

(Uh oh, wait a minute. I think I hear Dave running a bath!!! Splish, splash—that party may just have to wait! Cheers to a new year. I'm off to find my bathrobe—or not)!

*"There is absolutely nothing funny about
February.
It's like the 'f-word' of months."*
~Miss OMG

FEBRUARY

FOOTBALL FANDEMONIUM

Back in the day, you could count on professional football finally taking a hiatus toward the end of the January. Nowadays, this testosterone-ridden phenomena stretches into February—for reasons that have been explained countless times to me, but I can't seem to care enough about to remember.

All I know is that the Super Bowl is considered a holiday in my mostly male manor. I swear there are times that my family would serious contemplate giving up the presents of Christmas, the egg hunting of Easter, and the turkey dinner of Thanksgiving, if it meant the Super Bowl could be crowned an official American holiday.

(Author's Note: Please take heed that those same three males referred to above have indicated the "turkey thing" is a no-go, but they are definitely willing to give up Valentine's Day & Mom's Birthday as a solid substitute). Welcome to my world.

So football. Why football? I mean we start up in August and end seven months later. I'd say I could almost go through the entire "birthing process" in that amount of time—but let's get real—there is no tearing my husband away from the sports channel for anything more than to fetch a beer. So there's that.

At one point, I realized I could make my family's obsession with football more productive: Laundry. Yup, true story! I make them do the laundry. They can load/reload the washer and dryer during half times and mindlessly fold during commercial breaks. I love it! They get to watch their games and I don't have to slave away on the wash. It really is a beautiful thing.

Maybe we really should make the Superbowl a holiday?! Actually, for awhile there I was almost onboard with stretching football out to be a year round thing. But then I realized, there's always basketball. (Those games are worth a couple loads of laundry)! And then there is BASEBALL! Have you ever seen how long those games can go? I'm telling you friends—as long as there are professional sports going on all year

long, I will NEVER have to do the wash again.
GO TEAM GO!!!

~

IT'S THE THOUGHT THAT COUNTS (???)
Okay, so my incredible youngest son, gave me a
Valentine Card this year. It melted my heart
because I couldn't remember the last time he did
that.

So when I went to thank him and tell him how
special it made me feel, he replied, "I know. Oh,
and I used YOUR money to buy it—and I bought
Dad one too." Nice.

Valentine's Day is not a big deal in our house.
 Really. Further, I feign that I am okay with it—
basically because it is my fault that there's no
hoopla. You see, in the early days when I was
first married to that hunk o' burning love, (who I
am still hookin' up with), I realized early on that I
need to have very LOW expectations for days like
this—otherwise, I was just setting myself up to be
disappointed every year. I figured with that
thought process, I would just be ever so grateful
with whatever token of affection I received on this
over-glamorized holiday.

Boy, did that backfire! In order to carry out the plan, I knew I had to make numerous comments about him not needing to worry about getting me anything, because "I don't really celebrate. I'm just not big on this holiday." Well, crap! My husband actually took me at my word, for once. (How convenient—and selective, I might add)! Ugh.

So I brought it on myself, and I had to live with that—but what I didn't anticipate was I would later see that mentality did not serve as a good role model for our sons. (Now you know why they'd happily give up Valentine's Day for a turkey drumstick, if push came to shove). I pray for my children's future marriages. May their wives forgive me of my sins, and may they be able to retrain my boys to be better with their displays of affections. Good luck girls, (but, hey, at least they will do the laundry)!

~

FEELING FROSTED

February, in my humble opinion, seems to be the coldest month on Northern California. Thank gawd it is the shortest month of the year! (Cuz when it comes to cold weather, I'm a wimp)!
 Where we live, it's just cold enough to frost over

everything. It freezes pipes that will burst and cause utter disaster if not covered. It certainly makes you yelp when you sit on that thin layer of icy crystals on the commode first thing in the morning! But is does not actually snow. We are talking cold, but not "productive cold." We are talking iced over windshields, but no precipitation to ward off summer drought. Let's face it, we are talking it is cold enough that if you fart, snowflakes will shoot out your ass as you walk the dog on your morning stroll.

One day I decided I was done shivering, and ready for a little internal global warming to possess my body. I wanted a Spring Fever. Anything to warm my bones! So, I decided to take matters into my own hands. This relationship between me and Old Man Winter was just not working out. I decided to write a Letter of Complaint, a "Dear John Letter," if you will—and I wasn't messing around:

"Dear Winter,
I'm breaking up with you. Lately you've been giving me the cold shoulder, and our days together have been more dark & dismal, than a wonderland. Actually, I think our relationship was over before it even began. I hope that we can

be friends—snow skiing just wouldn't be the same without you.

Fondly,
OMG (aka: Miss Sunshine Girl)"

There was no response. I was completely iced out. Rumor has it that Winter heard I was spending my time with someone else: Summer. (What can I say? Do you blame me? Summer is totally hotter!)

The Mad Hatter: Have I gone mad?
Alice: I'm afraid so. You're entirely bonkers.
But I'll tell you a secret. All the best people are.
~Lewis Carroll

mARCH

MARCH MADNESS

I have learned that the March Madness is really not about what we all have always thought it was about. It has NOTHING to do with that sport where dribbling is okay and travelling is a bad thing—you know the one. Yep, basketball. And again, March Madness is not, I repeat, NOT about that.

Surprised? Imagine ours! As everyone knows, my family is full of sports fanatics, so basketball is on nonstop. (And when it overlaps with other sports—it gets a little crazy in the Giacomini Family). But that madness is also NOT what March Madness is about, (although sometimes I think it did get its names from the frustrating anguish that many proclaim while cursing their basketball "brackets."). Ridiculous really. I mean what did your brackets ever do to you? And I may have this wrong, but didn't you actually choose your own teams for those brackets? So really these fuming fellows should be bellowing at themselves. Right?

Anyway, March Madness really comes from the schizophrenia that encapsulates the month itself. First of all, there is that whole basketball thing. But we also have to survive March's little "on again, off again" behavior. I mean, sometimes there is Easter in March, and sometimes there isn't. Then there is the weather. In like a lion, out like a lamb. (Or is it the other way)? Lions? Lambs? All I know is I'm not too excited about seeing any lions outside my house. And sheep? Do NOT even get me started about those very baaa, baaa, baaad excuses for animals.

SIDENOTE: I grew up raising sheep. Long story, but the quick of it is I am absolutely not too fond of them. It's because they don't mind well, and they trample everything. Plus, word has it my parents used to make me go out to the pastures to play Bo Peep, just so they could be alone to "spin wool" inside. Whatever that means?

As if that wasn't enough, March also contains the craziest holiday ever. I mean come on! What other holiday would it be acceptable to celebrate a man in a funny outfit, while drinking lots and lots and lots of beer?

What? Oh yeah—forgot about Christmas and that Santa guy. I suppose that unofficial Superbowl holiday kinda counts too, under those parameters. So I guess the only difference is that whole "Kiss Me I'm Irish" thing. Oh hold on there—back to Christmas and mistletoe, (and that whole Valentine's Day extravaganza often follows with some smooching). Actually, now that I think about it, I believe I am retracting my original stance on this holiday. In fact, St. Patty's Day may be genius creation. It's sort-of a mix of all the best parts of the other holidays. It's MAD, I tell ya!

Ultimately though, with all the weirdness that is March, I actually know that March Madness is connected to the whole Winter-thing. No seriously! I have a theory that it stems from people getting cabin fever from freezing in frickin' February. For real! Old Man Winter drives people in the Northern Hemisphere so batshit crazy, that the second the sun begins to shine through in March, it triggers something deep within all humans. (At least the normal ones). It causes them to go, well, you know...mad! Mad at the fact they are sick of being cooped up and cold. Mad that there is NOTHING else on tv besides basketball. Mad that they may be stuck out in a cold, damp pasture watching a flock of sheep—while some adults are "flocking" indoors, and of course mad that they can't count on the weather—one moment it's beautiful and pleasant, the next it's a torrential cold-ass downpour.

March. It's madness.

"Finally. My winter fat is gone!
Now I have Spring rolls!"
~Author Unknown

APRIL

GOOD OLE EGG

We've always enjoyed celebrating Easter with the whole bunny thing. In fact, it was due to this particular bunny, that we realized our oldest may actually be fairly bright. He must've only been four years old or so when he asked how it was possible to have the Easter Bunny make it to all the kids' houses in time for egg hunting on Easter morning.

His thought, if memory serves me correct, was that this bunny couldn't possibly be THAT full of crap, in order to go around pooping eggs all over so many yards in the course of a morning.

What? I said he was bright. I never said he was a genius.

Or maybe he is, and his brother too! The pair seemed to find a way to get us to celebrate the yearly egg hunts in the most unique ways. We've found ourselves often on vacation during this time, or engaged in some super fun day trips somewhere. Their favorite was snowboarding on this sacred day.

Our boys didn't need baskets for egg hunting while snowboarding, but as luck would have it, the ski resort always had a snowboarding bunny who did! This bunny would slide gracefully down the mountainside, with a mass of crazy juveniles following close behind. That's because the bunny was carrying a huge Easter basket and was tossing eggs here, there and everywhere! I always marveled that the bunny didn't get blitzed by our boys, and the other manic minions, who were screaming and zipping themselves across the mountain, just to catch an egg. It was a downhill delight shared by all, for sure!

As our children got older, I found it sad not to have an egg hunt for them when they were at the Revolving Door Age. Just because we couldn't keep up with whether they were under our roof for a visit, or to set up camp once again, didn't seem like a reason to NOT to have the yearly hunt. But, they had lost their loving feeling—that is, until the year I hid beer bottles all over the yard!

Yep, nothing makes these boys bound for their baskets better than beer! But I decided there was a catch. Ah ha!

In order to scamper and scour the landscape for those tasty bottles of suds, they had to don some duds. So in their childhood Easter Baskets they discovered their mandatory garb: a hula skirt, a set of coconut shell bathing suit tops, Hawaiian Leis, and funky cartoon glasses.

It was quite a sight to see these two young men in this get-up—hysterical really to see them set off to find their rewards! But being the good sports they are, they did, and the only gripe was that the beers weren't cold—yet!

~

JUST A LOW DOWN SNAKE IN THE GRASS
We did have more gripes...or maybe "CRIPES!" at one of our huge egg hunts on our property out in the country, one year.

Out in the sticks, we have these things called "burn piles." Well, this one particular year we had a HUGE one—just tons of brush waiting for an official "Burn Day" for us to turn it into ash, and use in our garden. So after our youngest son decided to play Easter Bunny and go shower a couple acres of our property with candy-filled eggs, he and I decided we had just enough time to play a little joke on our unsuspecting guests.

For this egg hunt, we have certain eggs for the kids, and some special gold eggs for the grown-ups to find. The gold eggs go with some great gifts (think wine, and cool gifts as good as wine). Our youngest had a fake snake—a rubber cobra actually, that Dave and I used for a Halloween costumes some years back. So we found it and coiled it up near the huge brush pile and set a gold egg in the middle of the coil. Now what you also need to know is that we live in rattlesnake country. To be out in our pastures means not only are you searching for eggs, but you are keeping an eye open for those slithery creatures too! (And a burn pile just seems like the perfect place for them to hang out).

The egg hunt was on and we must've had 30+ kids and adults descending upon the pastures. The sounds of delight filled the air as eggs were being found left and right by the grown-ups—and the kids were having fun too.

Finally, one of our friends, Mr. Fish, began to close in on the burn pile. He must have seen a glint of the gold. As he approached the pile and the golden egg, there was a moment of realization that came over him as he began the motion to grab the egg. You could actually read what he registered, all over his face!

"SNAKE!" Mr. Fish jumped up and back so fast and so high, I thought that he may have been secretly training in Ninja techniques in his spare time.

We could hear him then question aloud, "Is that a real snake? Is that a REAL snake?" Of course we said nothing and continued to stifle our snickers.

As he allowed himself to move closer and closer to the imposter, he finally figured out the prank, grabbed the egg, and immediately looked up to us, as we began to release the hysterics of laughter we'd been holding back.

(I'm still waiting for the payback on that one, and according to his wife, it's going to be a beyotch)!

~

PRANKSTER PARENTING 101

Living in a house full of pranksters, it's always a glorious feeling when the first of April rolls around and I'm the one who pulls off a joke like

no other. (Probably because it rarely happens, since it's usually me who gets pranked).
I think I remember the first time someone ever really got me on April Fool's Day—it was my mom. She was out doing some weeding in our front yard, while the rest of us hid so we wouldn't be "guilted" into helping. Suddenly, we heard her barrel through the front door screaming "SNAKE!!!"

We lived in rattlesnake country there too—where you always watch your every step. I grew to be paranoid of stepping on a rattlesnake, because it was a very real threat, and those slithering things liked to visit our homestead ever so often.

So back to my mom's frightful screams…

As Mom let out her terrified exclamations, my dad flew out of his recliner so fast I thought he'd probably given himself whiplash—because I could hear him propel out and toward the front door clear from my bedroom, on the other side of the house. I then heard my sister's scrambling feet, while mine seemed to move underneath me without thought.

We all began hollering, "Where is it?" and running frantically with our hearts racing and adrenaline coursing through our bodies, toward our poor frightened mom, (who we thought was standing near the unwanted visitor).

That's when we saw her slowly, and dramatically, raise up her head that had been looking at the ground. She looked at each one of us and a giant grin began to stretch across her face as she ever-so-smuggly said to us, "April Fools!"

She got us! She got us good—but not without us hearing some new vocabulary terms muttered from our father's mouth.

Let's just say we learned a couple new things that day: a new level of curse words, and that we can't trust our mom—at least not on April 1st!

~

LIKE MOTHER, LIKE DAUGHTER

Following in my mom's footsteps, I've pulled off some great April Fools jokes in my time. Being a former elementary school teacher I would engage in a few classic moves, including writing the day's date as "March 32nd," just to see how long it would take the students to notice. I also stole a great one from one of my kids' teachers. We purchased these robin's egg candies that were being sold by a well-known coffee shop. They even came complete with a nest. The prank was so simple and so powerful—I'm surprised I didn't become a full-time prankster from the euphoria of the success.

Here's how it went down:

While transitioning between lessons, I told my 10/11 year old students I had something really cool to share with them for science that day. First, I grabbed a bag and very slowly & carefully reached in and pulled out the "nest." Next, I explained to the students that I had found it in my garden at home.

As I walked around the class to show each student the very precious and fragile nest, a few students became concerned that the mama bird was looking for it. But I was fast on my feet, for once, and shared that the nest had been abandoned, (shame on me), then when I got back to the front of the class I looked at the nest again in amazement, and gently lifted one of the eggs in the air, pinched between my thumb and pointer finger.

I asked the class, "Can you believe how small and delicate these eggs are?" I saw about 30 sets of eyes all on me.

As the class was nodding away, mesmerized by the sight, I bit the egg in half!

OH MY GAWD! The gasps of horror emitted from students was both awful and filled me with such pride at the same time. (Really warped, I know). You should have seen the disgusted looks on most of their faces. (I say "most" because some of the children actually took much glee from my chomp down on that egg—even more warped, if I do say so myself). Then I popped the rest in my mouth, chewed it up to sounds of "EWWWW!" and then said the words they were NOT expecting. (Yes, of course, "April Fools!"). The astonished looks and laughs beginning to brew were so great, that I made an encore performance the following year!

I will say, my students also learned a couple new things that day: 1) New vocabulary from their Language Arts lessons, and 2) They could never trust their teacher again—at least not on April 1st!

~

JUST FOOLIN' AROUND

So you may be wondering if any of my April Fool's antics have ever backfired? The answer is a resounding, "YES!" In fact, I recall more backfires than successes—but it never keeps me from trying again!

So one time I had a full-proof prank planned for my dear hubby. (It ended up failing, in theory, but it was still funny)! You see, with the help of my little friend, a small fake-but-looks-so-real snake, I set Dave up to stumble across this little guy in the kitchen. (Yes, there seems to be a theme with snakes and humor in our humble abode, and well, we always seem to live in snake country, so…).

Problem was, I sort of forgot about it and our youngest son went into the kitchen first. OH MYLANTA!!! I discovered my son has quite the vocabulary when it comes to expletives. (Guess it's all that bonding time with Grampa)!

With tears of laughter streaming down my face, I tried to stifle his rant-mixed-with-the-beginnings-of-his-laughter (as it was began to dawn on him what happened).

We quickly tried to recreate the situation before his dad walked in the door. Together we scurried off to the family room couch to sit in anticipation of Dave's entry. Suddenly, our unsuspecting victim entered the house, and began making his way to the kitchen. It took everything my co-

conspirator and I had to suppress our snickers and not peer into the kitchen to watch our loved one's every move.

So you are probably wondering what happened, right? Well, it took a while, but when my dearest, darling husband did see it, (being the "strong and silent-type"), we didn't quite hear him utter a verbal reaction, but there was a loud pause in his puttering around, and we swear he kicked it!

Best part: he thought it was my son's joke. To this day, I never told him it was mine.

Hey Dave, "April Fools!" (I guess I should probably watch my back now)!

~

FOOL ME ONCE, FOOL ME ~~TWICE~~ (STILL) ONCE

The ultimate time I had a joke that really backfired, it was both funny & not funny at the same time, twice.

Have I lost you?

Let me take you back in time when I was pregnant with our oldest son. It is important to note that I had a due date of May 8th with him. The reason that is important to know, is because earlier that year on April 1st, my co-workers and I decided to play a little joke with Dave and call him with the "Your wife's in labor" classic. Needless-to-say, he was NOT amused. He did not fall for it. And, again, he did NOT think it was funny, not in the least.

End of joke, right? Wrong!

Flash forward to later that month. April 29th actually. For a little background, I hate to admit that I had a co-worker who was a little on the annoying side. She was nice and all, so maybe it was my pregnancy hormones muddling my perception, (or the fact that she would corner me on my lunch break every single fricking day to discuss my pregnancy).

Now you may think that is very sweet that she had taken an interest. But her interest wasn't on how I was feeling, and how the baby was doing—she was more interested in my sex life and telling me how my husband and I should be doing the nasty, (with 8 months gestation going on under the carriage).

Every day, I would do everything I could to not respond and change the subject. But the lady was relentless! Seriously, she could have written a book on the Pregnancy Kama Sutra!

So given that, I began resorting to sneaking into the stairwell during my lunch hour and finding different floors with break rooms that I could hide out in—I mean no one wants to eat their bologna sandwich listening to all that baloney, right?

Well, at lunchtime on April 29th I began my daily disappearing act. As I set out climbing the stairs, I suddenly felt this little "whoosh." I knew EXACTLY what it was—I had peed my pants! OH MY GAWD! It happened! I read it in all the books that this could happen—and I swore it would never happen to me, and yet it did.

So now I am beyond embarrassed, and I decide I am going to drive home, change my clothes and come back (at least an hour drive, round-trip). I mean I had to, it was the end of the month, and I had quotas to make, and I was NOT going to sit in pee pee pants! To make matters worse, it was super busy for Dave too, he had some really intense meetings and projects to wrap up that week, as well, so I didn't even bother to call him to share my perplexing pissy problem. (He's welcome).

So I go home, change and then I get back to work. I am working away and realize I have this nagging pain in my abdomen. It was chronic, just kept happening over and over again. I would think it was going to go away and stop, and sure enough, it would come back again. UGH! I began thinking, "Am I getting sick? I don't have time to get sick. It's the end of the month!"

Finally, I started asking my co-workers, "Hey, is anyone feeling off? You know, sick? Like upset stomach or something?"

Everyone shook their heads "no."

"No cramping?"

Again, they shook their heads and began to look at me strangely.

Then my supervisor sauntered over and appeared at my desk to mention she thought maybe I was going into labor.

I was like, "There is no way! My due date is over a week away."

"I think you need to go to the doctor and get checked out."

I shook my head and replied, "I need to get my work done, I'm close to making quota so I don't want to stop to even call the doctor. I just want to make my month-end goals."

That's when the ~~nosy~~, (OOPS), I mean, "interested" coworker and another co-worker (mother of four), came over to my desk and started grilling me about my symptoms.

Suddenly, I started to realize that I didn't pee my pants, my water broke in the stairwell. OH MY GAWD! The one week that Dave & I needed to get through for work! The one week we were so stressed to wrap-up loose ends and finalize projects, before welcoming our new bundle of joy into our family! CRAPPPP!!!!

I quickly got on the phone and called the doctor's office. After going over my symptoms, they confirmed, "Um, YES, you should have come in hours ago to get checked out. Get here NOW!" I thought about driving myself, but my sane co-worker (and co-prankster caller from earlier in the month) told me I was INSANE, and that I needed to call Dave to come get me.

So I did.

He was not amused, he thought it was a joke, and he did NOT think it was funny—not in the least.

Words were strung together by him, as I explained to my dearest husband "it was time," like:

"Is this a joke?"

"This isn't funny, you know I have major projects due this week."

"Do you REALLY need me to come pick you up?"

It was that last sentence he uttered that made me shift from the dazed disbelief that "this is unbelievably happening" to absolute reality of "Oh my flipping GAWD, this IS HAPPENING!"

I believe my voice took on a tone between hysteria and stifled shrieking that Dave had never heard before, when I exclaimed, "NO, this is NOT a joke, GET HERE NOW!"

I hung up. I calmly collected my things and grabbed a box to pack away my belongings, (as I had planned a three month maternity leave). It was time.

Ten hours later, (I will spare you the gory details, because baby, giving birth ain't no joke!), our oldest came into this world. (And we've been laughing with him and his little brother—who arrived a year and half later—over their jokes and pranks ever since)!

Oh, and Dave...yep, he finally got me back for that awful April Fool's joke that year. Perfect timing, I might add: during the birth of our oldest.

It all happened when his initial shock wore off, and my ice chips were starting to melt. He began going into "coach-mode" to help me with my birthing breathing techniques. As he was reminding me of how to do my breathing, he began to blow his fast food Mexican meal into my face. Nice. NOT!

Needless-to-say, that didn't go over to well with me. I was not amused, it was NOT a joke, and I did NOT find it funny, not in the least.

"May is one Mother of a Month."
~Miss OMG

MAY

MOTHER'S DAY MAYHEM AT ITS FINEST
For years I dreamed of becoming a mom. While many of my Mother's Days are just a blur, there are some that stand out the most. Now it is important to note that I'm not a super "hearts and flowers" kinda gal. Don't need anything fancy for V-day, would prefer no one goes overboard for me at Christmas—because, despite their behaviors, my present is having my family together. (Usually). But let me tell you, there are two days a year that I expect to be celebrated: my birthday and Mother's Day.

Don't judge me. For all I do for my family, I deserve to be celebrated for my birthday—and for putting up with all their crap, they should throw me a frickin' parade for Mother's Day. And you know what? I would venture to say that most mothers out there deserve the same. C'mon people! Do you know a mother? Then show her some respect! (PS: If you are one of my kids, that goes TRIPLE for you)!

I honestly don't understand. Even though I have raised my kids to treat me like a queen on my Day of Honor, they still seem to be challenged in the execution of the pomp and circumstance. (To be perfectly honest, I actually think they could care less about this prestigious of holidays. I don't get it?)

I believe this because their presents usually suck. Yes, I said it—-there is just no sugar coating it. Seriously, with the exception of a couple years when they were tiny, and someone else was deciding what they were giving me, they really have stunk up the joint with their gift giving. Write me a letter, a poem, a joke—but don't give me something stupid. Clean the house, the bathroom—or at least your room, but don't be an idiot and think that you can re-gift me something you gave me last year. There's a reason it's still sitting in a closet under a layer of dust from non-use—it was a terrible gift!

Yep, I know, I sound like a total beyotch—completely ungrateful and all that. But here's the deal—you are RIGHT! And you want to know why? Let me share with you a typical Mother's Day gift from my dearest darlings:

I don't dream of expensive gifts—just ones that are thoughtful (of ME, not THEM)! I understand my children are not made of the big bucks—so there are times when I let them know that all I want is some physical labor for Mother's Day. (Yes, I am one of those "Acts of Service is Love" sorts of people). One of those things that screams, "I LOVE YOU, MOM!" is cleaning out the garage. Let's face it, I hate cleaning the garage, my husband hates cleaning the garage, and both of our kids certainly loathe it greatly. We get it—if we kept is clean, we wouldn't need to spend an entire day cleaning it out—but again, we hate cleaning the garage; thus, it tends to clutter, frequently!

So one year I gave advance notice, thinking the boys would be thrilled they wouldn't need to raid their piggy banks in order to present a present. I was super delighted to know that I would get to park my car in the garage Mother's Day evening, YAY!

I counted the days, the hours, the minutes that year. Finally, it was Mother's Day! HOORAY! I floated downstairs with glee to remind the guys they were helping me with the garage. Yes, I was pitching in too—quality family time! WIN-WIN!

No one hard-core complained over the reminder, so we were off to a great start. I got a bunch of, "I'll be there in a minute, gotta _____."

(Fill in the blank with an excuse of: eat breakfast again, take a dump, get dressed, find my other shoe, etc.). I knew these procrastination tactics. Hell, I invented them. But come on, it was Mother's Day, so there was no way they were going to leave me hanging. So I skipped on out to the garage and got started.

A couple hours later, and no kids in sight helping me, I was starting to get pissed. I marched into the house where I was showered with a new set of excuses: gotta eat lunch now, gotta take another dump, I forgot to get dressed, still can't find my shoe, and the real kicker, "What Mom? I was busy helping Dad." What the *BLEEP*?!

Thinking I laid on enough guilt, I returned to the garage, truly believing they were really following me this time.

Boy, was I wrong. Those little pain in the butts didn't show up until I was about 5 minutes away from completion. (Of course their story to you would be that they helped me clean the garage— on a technicality. You know what's worse? They did it again the next year. You'd think I'd learn?).

While we are speaking of technicalities, I should share about the year that I the shittiest gift EVER!

Yup, that would be the year it was super obvious that they didn't plan a single thing to commemorate this special day. I had given up on them and it was a gorgeous day. I wasn't going to waste the great weather, so I went out to the backyard to do some gardening. After about an hour or so of pulling weeds, my sweet cherubs emerged.

I was so excited thinking, "Wow! They are coming out to help me. YAY!" Wrong! They informed me quickly that they were, in no uncertain terms, not there to pull weeds, but that they needed to know where the wheel barrow was to bring me their Mother's Day gift.

What? A gift? A gift for Mother's Day? And how huge was this gift that it need a wheelbarrow to move it? I was giddy with anticipation! My boys were going to FINALLY step up! YAY!

A few minutes later, they began wheeling in nine bags of cow manure to me. "Here you go Mom, you said you needed this for your garden."

PEOPLE! I literally got shit for Mother's Day! And to add insult to injury—they charged it on MY credit card! I cannot win. Welcome to my life.

I am finally over this, I think. That's because I reamed them good for being awful to me. I reminded them of the crappy gifts they had given me in the past and told them they better straighten up or I would be repaying the efforts on their special days. I think that finally got though, because the next year, our oldest (who was away at college), really surprised me.

(He's actually very lucky to be alive from this surprise, as he snuck into the house at 3 in the morning and scared the hell out of me)!

Talk about a conspiracy. I had no clue—but glad I was worth the effort! Best Mother's Day gift ever to have all three of my favorite guys under the same roof!

Funny thing, I shared this story with some friends about how he crept in like a thief in the middle of the night and scared the daylights out of me, only to have a friend of mine shared with me it could have been much worse.

She said one time she snuck in to her parents' home, similar sort of deal, and the next morning she went to surprise them and opened their bedroom door to announce she was home. WELL! The surprise was on her, because she walked in on the two in the midst of doing the nasty-nasty! Talk about scarred for life! She said after that, she never surprised them with ANYTHING again!

YIKES!

I was thrilled that no scarring of lives happened, and that I didn't crack him over the head with a baseball bat, when he crept in the house. But even more, I was doing cartwheels because they were actually taking Mother's Day seriously, as they should, that year! My friends kept waiting for the other shoe to drop, cuz you know—we are talking about my kids here.

I was sure to give out frequent reports on my favorite social media platform all day, which finalized in this overall glimpse of the day:

MOTHER'S DAY REPORT-I can honestly say I didn't get sh*! this year...and we all know that's a good thing, considering my boys' track record! LOL!!! Great relaxing morning—incredible lunch with my favorite dessert—and a Trampoline Bouncy Ball game! WHOOHOO!!! I'll take it…(whatever it is). To top it off, the boys had a hiking trip planned, (which I love to do), but we are postponing for another weekend—because we all agree, this princess needs a nap! YAY! My boys really pulled through this year—I don't even have to go clean the garage! Wow! I guess they are growing up!!!

One of my friends, who's also the mother of two boys, (slightly younger—the boys, not the friend, I'd like to point out), was thrilled! She exclaimed, "So there's hope?!?! Please tell me it's so!"

I immediately responded, "At least a glimmer! (And that's no shit)!"

~

THE PERILS OF POST MOTHER'S DAY DEPRESSION

I feel so fortunate to have a wonderful day, like Mother's Day, all devoted to treating ME kind. Like many moms out there, I do so much for my family the other 364 days of the year, so it's nice to have a "Me Day," and not have to feel guilty about it.

Regardless of the quality of the final product, I can usually count on being treated a little better than usual on this most ceremonious of days. To recap: it usually begins with a ridiculously early wake up call of breakfast being shoved at me, while I attempt to sit up in bed and not spill everything on the covers (for which I would inevitably be the one who'd need to clean up). As previously referenced, this is usually followed by a mandate from the queen on some manual labor to be done without gripage. (I would be playing the role of the queen in this scenario, and yes, I made up the word "gripage," meaning the spewing of such gripes from children in protest of having to get off their butts and do something physical). Later in the day, gifts of chocolate bars, sometimes a card and dinner is prepared for me. Not too shabby—I'll take it. (Remember, it's a lot better than the year they HONESTLY got me cow manure for Mother's Day).

But what I HATE about Mother's Day is the day following it. That's right. The very next day, every single year, I get PMDD, Post Mother's Day Depression. It's a clinical phenomena and I understand I am not the only one it affects.

Haven't heard of PMDD? Well, allow me to explain. You see, after a day of pampering, (whatever that may look like—for me that means getting some help with cleaning the previously mentioned garage), the Monday after Mother's Day is a big ole slap of reality, right upside the head! It's the decline from the high one has been on the previous day, to returning to the low of the normal daily grind.

That's right, still woken up early, but instead of by one's obstinate offspring, it an annoying alarm clock. Of course then one has to drag herself off to her regular day of whatever work it is she does. No one attempts to make breakfast for you, and you're forced to pour your own milk in your oatmeal. Geez, not fair!

Kids are back to ignoring you at full throttle and grouchiness is back to an all time high. No asking them to do something without hearing, "I'll do it later…" or the one that really pisses me off, "Gawd, Mom, we worked all day on the garage yesterday, just for you. Now you want me to take the trash out too?" Of course they never stop without this precious zinger: "CRIPES MOM, you make me do everything. You are so ungrateful." *deep cleansing breath here, before I smack the crap outta him*

Then of course by evening, it's back to cooking for the family and cleaning up everything. And the ultimate worst part of PMDD is the weight gain. Since I'm a chocoholic, it never fails that I get chocolate for Mother's Day—problem is the chocolate is completely gone by the following night, and I've eaten every bit of it, ALL BY

MYSELF!!! (Guess I forgot to mention. One of the symptoms of PMDD is stress eating, ugh! And I must admit, when it comes to chocolate, I'm not known for being a good sharer). It goes without saying, this is now coupled with the depressing dread of stepping on the scale the next day, just to be doomed by those delectable delights. Definitely a downer.

But the silver lining is that in 364 days, I will be Queen of the Castle again for 24 hours, so that one thought alone gives me something to look forward to. Now go eat some chocolate!!!

*"We wondered why when a child laughed, he belonged to Daddy.
And when he had a sagging diaper that smelled like a landfill,
'He wants his mother.'"*
~Erma Bombeck

JUNE

FESTIVE FATHER'S DAY FOLLIES

When June rolls around, so does summer in Northern California, and along with it comes the beloved holiday of Father's Day. YAY!

There are a lot of truths about Father's Day that most think, (especially mothers), but would never say out loud. Guess, what? The jig is up. I'm going to put it out there! I am going to blab it all. And I'm going a step further—I'm putting it in writing! (Now if that doesn't show you I've got some big cajones, I don't know what would).

Here's the best kept secret, and it is really intended for ALL those dads out there. There is a reason that Father's Day falls after Mother's Day, (and soon thereafter, I might add). It's because we moms are smart—and you can best believe that it was probably a jilted, GENIUS mom who etched that Father's Day date in stone!

You see, we take stock of what actually goes down on Mother's Day with a full assessment of the day. We measure the total success of the day against a rubric that no one has ever divulged before—and you dads have never seen it, because the rubric is committed to memory. So there's no evidence of its existence. But trust me, it's there!

My guess is you are probably wondering what is measured? Well, get ready—because this just became a "Tell All" book. So buckle up people, here we go:

INSTILLED IMPORTANCE-First we take into account the age of the children and how much their father has instilled the importance of celebrating their mother. Rating systems can vary, but I use the 1-10 rating scale.

1 = Dad is a total d-bag and completely forgot, thus the little tots didn't have a chance in hell to please mom on her special day
10 = Dad of the Year has planned with the little one(s) for months every little detail from dawn to dusk on making this year's day even more amazing than the last

(Yes, a 10 in this area is practically impossible to achieve—but hey, goals)!

CREATIVE CONTENT-The next area of importance is how the day unfolds. What did this lovely family plan for their beloved mother?

1 = Tossed a granola bar at her, smacking her in the head, (nearly putting an eye out), while waking her up from a dead sleep—oh, and calling it "Breakfast in Bed."
10=Day breaks and the cherubs are stealthily creating a masterpiece culinary delight, as their mother slumbers sweetly. With no fuss, they wait patiently for her to awake...naturally...before enthusiastically bombarding her with breakfast. The days continues, (with a clean house), never causing the mom to lift a finger to work, and is a true full day of pampering. Further they shower her with thoughtful gifts, that suit HER interests. (Yes, most fall somewhere in the middle. But that's okay, it's a start and allows room for improvement, right)?

SPECIALNESS FACTOR-This may seem redundant, but there really is a difference. It's about sincerity—because a mom can tell! This is actually a great way to score more points— especially if the kiddos are strapped for funds!

1 = Low to no effort made &/or gift given but with no thought of the recipient. (Example: Monster Truck Rally tickets, Gift Card to the local gas station, No Show on Garage Clean-out Duty) 10 = Grandest gesture possible under the circumstances. (Example: Finger painting with "World's Best Mom" written across the paper, Snuggling in front of a movie—letting Mom pick the flick, "I Love You to the Moon & Back" hugs).

Just saying, we know.

When the rubric is calculated, a final score is determined. This is important, because it is this outcome that determines Father's Day. That is right! Whether you want to admit it or not, the gestures given on Father's Day are 9 times out of 10 a direct correlation to what went down a month earlier (according to me and my research).

Yep, now you dads know, so there's no more excuse! Start early, start young, and make a strong showing! Cuz your special day is pending that final tally!

Now that I've let you in on that little secret, I'm ready to divulge another. This one is for the moms out there helping to plan those special Father's Days. Here's the scoop, in order to plan the perfect Father's Day, you need to think of what that day is really all about. I say it's all about said dad spending LOTS & LOTS of quality time with his children. In order to do that, he really needs to have LOADS of time to focus on just them. So, being the thoughtful mother that I am, I go out of my way to plan out those special days.

I have helped my two boys secure tickets to baseball games—just a party of three with no me. Oh bummer. The three of them off having a great time, while I find myself alone. Yes, all alone in a quiet and clean house, with the remote all to myself, (while praying for extra innings).

I've also sent my children to celebrate with their dad, and both of their grandfathers for an ultimate day long adventure of waterslides. (This celebratory event caused both my own mother and mother-in-law to have to fill their alone time. You're welcome Mom & M-I-L!). I must admit, this one backfired a tad on me, as I expected them home around 4 or 5pm that evening—and they showed up at the house early—guess they wore the grandpas out! (So much for that massage I had scheduled to help pass the time).

These were definitely some of my finer Father's Day plans—but I would have to say that the ultimate Father's Day gift I planned was the one when I left town at 4:30am on a Father's Day, for a week. Yes, it was super selfless act, allowing my children and husband to have a week of togetherness to celebrate him and bond. Wasn't I thoughtful? Yep, and a few other father's benefited from it too, because three of my girlfriends join me. It was rough! We had to seek solace with each other as we were forced to soak up the summer sun & slurp down the suds on the beaches of the Mexican Riviera—all in the name of father-child bonding.

The things we do to ensure our kids' fathers have an awesome day of spending time with them. It's a sacrifice really…(a genius sacrifice, that is)!

"If laughter is the fireworks of the soul,
Be careful telling jokes while eating beans!"
~Miss OMG

JULY

BOOM-CHICA-NO BOOM!

For the life of me, I do not understand the appeal of blowing up stuff to celebrate momentous occasions. Don't get me wrong, I do love fireworks, (now)...but I just don't get the point for celebrations?

It probably stems back to when I was a very little girl and my parents took me to The Stadium to see the annual fireworks show. I HATED IT! Every. Single. Second. I was frightened of the noise that reverberated throughout my body with each boom. I screamed and cried and threw a frickin' fit! All I wanted to do was go home to our little farm, and be blanketed by the peace and quiet of the cows.

My parents were so exasperated with me. I'm sure they thought this was going to be a phenomenal treat. It probably cost them a pretty penny to take me to this extravaganza, too. At one point, they were so frustrated with me, they

told me if I didn't like it I could just walk home.
(Let's be honest, that's what my little ears
thought I heard through all that loud, crazy noise.
However, I'm sure there's a thread of truth to this
memory—because it sounds like something I
would have said to my own kids!). Anyway, I
was okay with that challenge, I just wanted the
Hades outta there, so I got up and started walking,
hands clamped over my ears the whole way.

The "whole way" was walking along the upper
deck walkway of The Stadium. And let's be real,
I was about four or five years old. There was no
such way I knew how to walk home from where
we were. Hell, I didn't even know where our car
was, and I think at that age I still thought my
mom's name was "Mom."

I do remember as I was walking and walking
trying to drown out the awful booms, that a
firefighter walked up to me and asked me where I
was going, and if I needed help. I point blank told
him I was going to the car and I didn't need any
help. (I may have asked him to stop the show,
however. That part's a little fuzzy.) I remember
that he looked a little puzzled, and then he looked
up over my head and gave a knowing look. Sure
enough, my mom had trailed behind my li'l Miss
Independent soul. I remember feeling perplexed

at that moment, glad that my mom cared enough
to be sure I wasn't abducted as I stormed off, but
a little pissed that she didn't think I could find my
way home on my own! Geez, Mom! Ye of little
faith in a five year old.

Needless-to-say, I still didn't enjoy the show, I
still hate loud noises today—and for the rest of the
time we lived on that farm, Fourth of Julys were
spent watching the fireworks from our pastures,
(at least 10+ miles away from The Stadium...and I
loved it)! Nothing screams "Freedom" better than
the silent shimmer of red, white and blue
glittering in the air, as we listened to the cows
moo in the moonlight. Just sayin'.

~

THERE JUST WASN'T A
REAL SPARK BETWEEN US

I was preteen before I was ever exposed to the
firecrackers you could buy at the fireworks stands.
 I always felt they were a little lackluster—and
some were also annoyingly loud, so there's that.

Surprisingly, I did have a few favorites. There
were these spinning rosettes that I was particularly
enamored with—that is, until one got stuck under
a car. I was totally freaked out that the car was

going to blow up! No longer a fan—thank goodness those are now banned.

However, I do love the old Bottle Rockets—those were cool. Just a hum of a swoosh and a quiet pop before the pretty sparkles! Yep, I think those are banned now too. (At least in my neck o' the woods).

For sure though, I cannot stand the regular ole firecracker—the light & boom kind. Hey! Those could blow a finger or two off! I should know!

You see, I used to be a lifeguard at our community lake for several years until I was almost 20. After a very long day of hollering, in the blistering California sun, at kids (& some dumbass grown-ups) one Fourth of July, I drove 20 minutes to meet up with my boyfriend. (For the record, he was older than me). He happened to be attending a party at his neighbor's house. Well, needless-to-say, while I spent the day working my butt off yelling and policing the lake, he must've spent the day doing the exact opposite, because he was in a sloppy good mood.

The reason I was there was because we were fixin' to go, believe it or not, to a fireworks show. YES! I know what you are thinking—but this show was choreographed to music—music makes everything better, right?

So, considering his state for our date, I OBVIOUSLY needed to drive. As we got close to the venue, he got really excited. When I asked what was going on, he reached down between his legs and pulled up a strand of firecrackers.

"Lookie here!" he joyfully exclaimed.

I did NOT share his enthusiasm. I instructed him to put them away because I didn't like them and I didn't want them in my car. Being the gentlemen that he was in that moment, he decided to ignore me, and light a few to throw out the window. Yes, you read that right. But, in his state of mind, he thought it would be smarter to throw them out MY window—while I was driving. WTFrick?!

Oh! But there's more. As he went to throw the lit firecrackers, they bounced back in and onto my bare-skinned lap. (Guess it didn't occur to him the my window wasn't rolled down enough for him to engage in his activity). As I screamed and tried desperately to control my stick shift car, I believe I call him every freaking word in the book as each firecracker exploded, burning into my skin. Pain seared through my lap, while anger and tears raged my face. It was a living nightmare. Still driving, I made my way to a convenience store, where Mr. Dumb Bunny decided he should probably be the one to go in and get me a bag of ice for my lap. (Ya think)?

It's been decades since that day, and while I have forgiven him, I will never forget—and I still have the scars to remind me in the event I almost do.

And you wanna know what's really perplexing? Right now I know some of you are feeling my pain...and some of you thought this was funny (kinda like those students who cheered when I chomped the egg). Yep, you know who you are!

MORAL TO THIS STORY: Fireworks explosives are not for child's play. So, let the grown-ups, who've been tossin' back cocktails all day, set them off. (Geez)!

~

LIFE'S LESSONS LEARNED, OR NOT

Well, I've learned that lighting fireworks must be a "guy thing," because my husband, (who was NOT the boyfriend in exploding-firecrackers-in-the-car scenario), loves them too. There's nothing like the Fourth of July to bring out his Inner-Pyro—and our two boys are just like him.

In fact, when I've asked our kids about their most memorable Independence Days, it isn't swimming or BBQs, nor time with cousins that sparks their best memories. It's the time they got to buy what they'd like to believe were "illegal fireworks" on their very favorite childhood vacation ever.

Funny thing is, they were actually on an out-of-state vacation with their Uncle & Auntie, without their dad and me, and the fireworks were only illegal in our state—not where they were visiting. So hate to burst their little 5 minutes-of-hell-raisin'-moment-bubble, but they were legit as sh!+! So kiddos, the truth is out—guess you aren't quite the bad boys you thought you were! (Furthermore, I am firmly going to believe that it was the fireworks, (not the "sans mom" part), that made that trip their favorite).

~

PATRIOTIC PARENTING

As married adults, my husband and I often find ourselves on vacation during the Fourth of July week. Mostly because I would be off work, and the company my husband worked for used to shut down for the week. (Mandatory vacation). While some of the vacations were out of the country, other times we would find ourselves in unique settings in The States—like hilltop fireworks watching with our family in Georgia, or over the lake in Tahoe.

But the Independence Day vacation I remember most was the summer after 9/11. It was one of those "right place at the right time" kinda moments. During a trip to the east coast to visit friends in Pennsylvania, and family in Maryland, we were able to make our way to New York City. On the Fourth, we walked from our hotel off Times Square, down to JFK Blvd, to watch the fireworks over the harbor. (Maybe there was some subway taking too, but I just remember walking, and walking, and walking some more). Friends and family thought we were nuts, especially after what had happened less than a year before. Much of our country was still fearful, and even more still mourning. To pay tribute, we had visited Ground Zero earlier in the day so our sons could see where the terror had transpired.

I'm not sure at what age someone begins to feel the sense of patriotism in their bones for their country. I think it may be different for everyone. And while I cannot say if patriotism took a hold of my children that day, I can say it tugged at my husband, and me. I, for one, never felt more

American than that night as we all watched, and "oohed and ahhed" over the symbolic bombs bursting in air. Our nation had been gutted months earlier, but that night we all stood united, and proud, and strong. God Bless America!

Now THAT sort of celebrating with fireworks I get. So go light a sparkler and celebrate people!

"Oh bummer, it's the first day of school."
~Said no parent EVER!

AUGUST

GO FORTH & BE EDUCATED

While many mourn the last of the summer days in North America this month, more can be found rejoicing.

That's because an unofficial holiday takes place in much of the USA—BACK TO SCHOOL!

It's true. Around this time of year, parents of school age children begin to smile more with every passing day. They suddenly begin to get a little spring in their step, and the closer it gets to the first day of school, some are almost floating on air.

"Why?" you may ask.

Because they are tired. For those who do not work with children, it can be an exasperating feat to completely have one's children in their own care for so many weeks at a time.

(There is a reason our educators should be paid more in our country—they have your children most of the year)!

Think of it this way: most parents have their hands full enough with their own kids. Try imagining that you are hosting a slumber party with 30+ kids. You need to take care of each child and attend to their individualized needs: gluten allergies, peanut allergies, afraid of the dark, fearful of dogs/cats/hamsters/the dark/you-name-it, must take meds at precise times, etc. The list can go on and on, right? Next, add in keeping them focused and entertained so they don't destroy your home. Now, try doing that for approximately 180 days a year, more or less.

(It's okay, I know I lost most of you at "slumber party with 30.")

So, let's just agree that teachers are amazing—and you should be kinder to them. I mean, 180 days to your few weeks? C'mon!

Okay, back to parents tearing out their hair... When we are in the depths of winter, or even in the early stages of spring, it is easy to somehow daydream about the sweet summertime right around the corner. Long, lazy days. Slowing down and enjoying each others' company. Fun adventures and memories of lifetime to be made.

But then reality sets in like a big ole punch to the gut. And as if that weren't brutal enough, it usually sets in on the day we tend to look forward to the most...the LAST day of school! That's right. Come the minutes after the last day of school, when no projects need to be created, no homework to be done, no studying for the next day's test...and suddenly, there's a whole lot of time on your hands, (and that equates to a ton of time on your kids' hands too)! And it doesn't take long for that extra time to snowball!

I can sum up the biggest challenge of this predicament into two words, (and YES, like chalk screeching across a chalkboard, they are the two words every single parent in the world shudders to hear). Hand on heart, I swear those words come like clockwork, and always arrive less than 24 hours after the classroom door smacks them on their li'l behinds on their way out. Yep, that's when these sweet cherubs complain, "I'm bored."

"I'M BORED?" "I'M BORED!" They haven't had enough time to be bored!

Seriously, can there be two worst words in the world? NO! At least not when combined together, and the reason is simple: it becomes an instant kick in the booty that all your dreams of summertime bliss are about to bomb.

Suddenly all the lazy days of summer dynamics have shifted and in a panic, parents scramble to plot a new plan!
I always called mine: "PLAN KEEP'EM OUTTA MY HAIR."

Here's how the plan worked:

First I devised a strict routine.
Kids were expected to sleep in and go to bed early. Too bad that the sun is still up at 9pm, that's what sleep masks are for!

First thing in the morning we went over the "afternoon chores," for when they are done playing. I liked to hang this over my boys' heads with an early reminder so that maybe they'd stay outside playing longer.

Lunchtime was a quick grab and go back to playing over at their friends' houses sort of thing, followed by (as hinted) play dates carefully scheduled daily for weeks upon weeks. Evenings were always jam-packed with sports' practices. So my kids got lots playtime, some accountability lessons and exercise. And you know what? They still had the nerve to utter that awful phrase! The ingrates!

What makes it worse, if you have more than one child, is that only a couple of weeks in and they are already sick and tired of each other. (I get it, because, quite frankly, I am sick of them too)! While striving to master the challenge of getting on each others' nerves at the highest degree, my children also succeeded in driving me crazy!

That is, until the day I instituted "Cooperation Lessons."

Now don't get me wrong, these lessons were not fool-proof, but they worked most of the time. My kids hated them as much as I despised the words, "He's bugging me!"

I bet you're probably wondering what Cooperation Lessons are right about now, aren't ya?

Ok, allow me to share a few examples with you:

One of my all-time favorites is "Dynamic Duo Floor Scrubbing!" Yep, made my kids get on the floor and hand scrub it. Nope, it didn't take long before they agreed to get along for the rest of their lives—well, until next time (which was always the next day).

Then there was "Bathroom Cleaning Buddies!" I'm sure you can imagine two boys cleaning up their own pee off the ground and scrubbing the toilet. That'll teach'em for messing with my Summer Sanity.

And of course, "Laundry Lads!" This one was actually a very useful one for them, as they learned at a very young age how to do their own damn laundry. (Again, you are welcome future spouses of my children).

So cooperate they did—sometimes. At least long enough for me to sneak away and get a Mother's Little Helper (aka: much needed batch of margaritas for two—that I drank solo. What? Don't judge! They were for medicinal purposes, of course—haven't you ever heard of "take two and call me in the morning?" It's a motherhood survival remedy.). I mean something's you just don't mess with.

In fact, that last tip works so well, that about two and half weeks into Summer Break, (along with a pair of ear plugs from the dollar store), and it's Buh-bye Boredom and hello pool time—because quite frankly I've now reached the state of "stay outta my hair, cuz this mama don't care!"

(PS: Even though I was a school teacher most of the years I raised my kids, truth be told, I, too, looked forward to the First Day of School, when THEIR teachers would take THEM, and I could have a well-deserved break with my 30 attendees at our daily slumber party. I mean, at least my students never said they were bored)!

"If you're born in September,
chances are your parents started off their new
year
with a bang."
~Author unknown, but seriously?
This is something no September baby EVER wants
to know!

SEPTEMBER

HAIL TO THE HELL MONTH

In the good ole U.S. of A there is a holiday that occurs toward the beginning of the month. It's called "Labor Day." The special day is intended for honoring the American Labor Movement and the contributions that workers have made to the strength, prosperity, laws, and well-being of the country.

That is great and all—power to the people! But in our family, September's Labor Day means something different. Now for the record, I am not dismissing the intent of the holiday—I am simply sharing the extended version of this well-respected holiday.

When I was very young, the holiday, (in my brain), stood for the "Last Hurrah" before school started—because back when the earth was cooling, school started the day after Labor Day in our state. (I think enough "hung-over, exhausted-from-spending-the-entire-day-at-the-lake" parents finally won that battle and were able to compromise to have school start two weeks earlier. Why earlier? I do NOT know—but those are thoughts for another book).

The "school thing" pales in comparison though, because in our family Labor Day represents a "different kind of labor." You know the kind that involves a females squeezing, pushing and cursing a kid through her vaginal region. Yes. I just said that. Get over it.

So Labor Day and giving birth are what we celebrate in our family—but we affectionately refer to it as "Hell Month." That's because we have five members of our family (at last count), who celebrate their birthdays in that month.

I hear many people have families with this same problem—and YES, it is a problem! When you are celebrating your mom, your uncle, pseudo-brother-in-law-otherwise-known-as-your-sister's-baby-daddy, your husband and your OWN birthday, it's just exhausting thinking about it—let alone to celebrate!

But no worries, cuz you better believe we will celebrate, as there will be hell to pay, if we don't. (So if my kids are reading this, take note: DO NOT THINK YOU ARE OFF THE HOOK!!! Take it to heart, take out a loan, or take time to finger paint some "World's Best (insert family member here)" pictures! Regardless, suck it up kiddos. Hell Month comes once a year. So basically, when October rolls around, it's time to start planning for next year's September Birthday Marathon! Or else you are out of The Will!)

THE WILL: Okay, that is hysterical right there. I love telling my kids they need to be careful, because they are currently in my Will. We often remind them that it is to their advantage to be sure their dad and I live a very long and healthy life, because all they are going to inherit is our humongous mountain of debt! Needless-to-say, our kids engage in welfare calls & visits for us frequently.

At first, I just thought they were becoming the most caring and thoughtful young men in the world—that is until I found out they were just nervous about paying off our bills. Whatever, damn li'l brats. After all we've done to raise them, the least they could do is throw us a bonus! I mean can you imagine how rich we would be if they tipped us for every diaper change, or when I did the ole "fill'er up" expressing milk from my boobs 'til they felt they were going to be sucked completely off my body? It's horrible, right? Their Auntie Z always referred to it as "Milking her Cows." (She has twins—so double the trouble). Ow.

Can you imagine bonus pay for every sleepless night of taking care of them? How about differential pay for being up all night with them while they were running fevers? What about stress pay for making us worry so much? And while we are on the subject, how about considering mileage reimbursement for all the frickin' chauffeuring we did their WHOLE. ENTIRE. CHILDHOOD?

I mean come on! If we actually charged our kids for the hours, the pain & the suffering we went through to bring them into this world & keep them in it, well, quite frankly—the total's rather astronomical. So I am thinking they owe us big.

Luckily for Dave & me, our kids have a whole extra day to prepare to celebrate their us BIGTIME, when they enjoy the day off from

work each year, on the first Monday of
September.

~

DON'T FALL FOR IT~PART 1

In Late September, a special day occurs that has
nothing to do with gestation occurring in a mature
female's body. Nope, this one is seasonal. It's
the transition of summer to autumn. According to
the calendar, it is supposed to happen overnight.
WHAT A JOKE! Right around September 22/23
each year, everyone in my neck of the woods
expects to shed their flip flops, tank tops and
short-shorts overnight for sweaters, jeans and
scarves.

Guess what? Each year, with great anticipation,
we wake up in gorgeous, sunny Northern
California to 80+ degree days and we pull on the
jeans, sweaters and scarves—just to ditch them by
noon for our flip-flops and bikinis before we go
plunge into the pool for an afternoon of extended
summer fun in the sun. EVERY. SINGLE.
YEAR. The darn excellent weather! It's a curse
really.

You would think we'd learn? I mean seriously.
This year I voted in shorts and summer sandals—
on Election Day!

*"A couple goes to an art gallery.
They find a picture of a naked woman with only
her privates covered with leaves.
The wife doesn't like it and moves on, but the
husband keeps looking.
The wife asks: 'What are you waiting for?' The
husband replies: 'Autumn.'"
~Jokester Unknown*

OCTOBER

PULPY FICTION

I don't get it. What's the appeal of stealing someone's pumpkin and smashing it all over the street? PUMPKIN PEOPLE—this is an injustice! Think of all the pumpkin pies that will never be, because of these thoughtless hoodlums! (Hmm, less pumpkin pies = less calories going straight to my thighs—on second thought, maybe I should thank these li'l pumpkin punks)!

Seriously though, pumpkins take a lot of work to transform into the artistic jack-o-lanterns they become. Right? I mean hollowing out these gooshy gourds is hard enough. Then there is the painstaking, time consuming carving of that pumpkin. Depending on who is doing the carving this could be several minutes of slice and dice...or hours and hours of serious sculpting. They really are a work of art, right? And would you be okay with someone splattering your Michelangelo, your Rembrandt, your Monet all over the streets? I think not! I mean, come on! You probably haven't even gotten all the goo out from under all your fingernails from all the time you spent transforming your pumpkin into a masterpiece. In fact, the smell is probably still permeating from your skin, as the pieces lay strewn all over the sidewalk.

The ghouls!

I shared my chagrin about terrible treatment of our super squash on social media, and quickly discovered many others have the same thought—expect one. A stand-alone comment of "smack my head proportions." (It's comical really, because I cannot remember the exact words my fellow "agreers" had, but I can totally remember the one who didn't)!

"Well, Miss OMG, vandalizing aside, the pumpkins we generally buy for jack-o-lanterns are not that good for pies."

Really? That's your point? Are you really lacking in support of these poor defenseless squash? 'Cuz it sounds like you are? AND, furthermore, how do you know which sort of pumpkin I bought? And who says I cannot turn my pumpkin purchase into pie, or bread or soup or one of the many other wondrous culinary treats I love some much? Lady! Either get on the pumpkin wagon or go plop your pumpkin somewhere else, cuz in this neck o' the woods we do not discriminate against our various pumpkin pals!

Yeesh!

Furthermore, Pumpkin Punks, respect others' and don't squash their squash, dammit!

You know what? I am beyond pissed over this pumpkin pulp, so out of respect for my neighborhood, I am no longer buying a "real pumpkin" for display. Instead, I shall stick with reusable plastic pumpkins. Less fuss, less muss. (You're welcome neighborhood)!

~

   MIND YOUR MANNERS AT MY MANOR! It must be the over-dose of pumpkin spice that causing people to lose their minds and forget their manners on October 31st. I hope that isn't true, because I am a pumpkin spice FREAK!!! (Love it all, seriously: lattes, bread, muffins, coffee, yogurt, bagels. Yes, yes, yes, I truly love it ALL—the more pumpkin spice the better. I mean it isn't the weather that makes autumn so awesome, it's the PUMPKIN SPICE)!!!

But something happens in late October that affects the kids. Some go a little nuts on Halloween and jack up our hi-jacked Jack-o-lanterns. But even hours before that I've noticed a phenomenon that almost makes me want to turn off the lights and hide inside on Halloween night. It's the lack of politeness.

Every year our family gets a little giddy as we look forward to answering the door to voices singing out, "Trick o' Treat!" Personally, I love seeing all the great costumes and the smiling faces, as parents hover close-by.

I also LOVE the kids that have been taught manners! Because lately, there aren't many out there. So sad to report, I'm about ready to break out the boxes of raisins and carrot sticks.

One year it began to seem a little aggressive even. One of my nearby neighbors shared that most of the kids didn't even bother to utter the traditional words "Trick o' Treat," they just stuck out their bag for candy—like they were accepting an entitled hand-out or somethin'. Some got to grabbing, with their grubby hands, into the candy bowls like gremlins. It was ghastly!

My sister said she had 10 very polite tots come to the door using their best manners. But that has me a little perplexed. On one hand, I like to think that means there is hope for future trick o' treaters, but on the other, it is kinda sad that she could actually keep count of the only polite visitors who came a knocking.

I was more appalled when, I swear, I had a kid look at me and accost, "What about me?"
Hell, I figured the kid was chaperoning the little ones. She had NO BAG, and there was no "Trick o' Treat." I had to actually cue her on what to say.

Then she responded real snotty, "I just take it in my hand."
Take it in my hand? WTF does that mean?
PRIMA DONNA!!!

OMG!!! These kids scare me. No gratitude, just rudeness. I just want to scream at these people's parents: TEACH. YOUR. KIDS. MANNERS. DAMMIT.

And seriously, what the hell do you do when you give out a handful of candy to a swarm a 4 year olds, just to have them then say, "I want to pick!"?

What??? I mean their picking is their grabbing of tons more candy that is intended for the next several groups of goblins getting ready to ascend on my doorstep. They are only four? How much candy can they possibly devour?

It becomes a vicious cycle really, because that means handing out the budget candy, and with budget candy you get the awful comments of, "Are you kidding me?"

It's true...hand on heart it has happened to me! And it takes everything I have to bite my tongue and not say, "Spread the word you li'l creep and don't come back to my house again until you find your frickin' manners." But I don't because I don't want my pumpkin to take the hit for me losing my gourd on some foul mouth fairy princess who can't bother to carry a flippin' bag!

I guess I should look at the bright side: maybe there is a new NO BAG movement. I hear my nephew did the same. Maybe it's a "Save the Environment" kind of thing, or maybe a way to cut down on the sugary treats for a healthier lifestyle. I don't know what it is—(but it is just weird)! My gawd, when I was a kid we were already upcycling! Talk about being environmentally friendly. We took pillowcases with us and it was our goal to come back with them full. That's right, we were watching out for Mother Earth & we were goal setting! Yep, and that's not all—because you best bet we brought our manners too!

~

IT MAY BE TIME TO CALL IT QUITS

Some have shared with me that they think when a child is old enough to shave the child needs to call it quits with Trick o' Treating. I disagree whole-heartedly and say, "Hey, bring it on!"

I'd much rather have these kids out trick o treating than to have them getting into other mischief.

I believe both of my boys were still trick or treating in 12th grade! (And rumor has it, it transitions to Trick o' Drinking in college). One of my sons wore the same dang costume over and over for years. I even remember the year when he realized it was his last hurrah to get away with going trick o' treating. It was bittersweet—his swansong of annual begging. I was totally supportive, but you best believe I had "the manners talk" with him before he left!!! (Seriously I did, before he drove off to go door to door. Because we all know I would kick his a$$ to the frickin' moon and back if I found out he didn't use his manners! So if anyone had a rude cow drive up and visit them on Halloween, let me know, 'cause Miss OMG don't play those games)!!!

*"In the USA, elections are held in November,
Because it's the best time for picking out a
turkey."*
~Author unknown

NOVEMBER

DON'T FALL FOR IT~PART 2

The day after I voted, (while comfortably clad in shorts and flip-flops, I might add), Autumn decided it was ready for its yearly arrival.

This had me scouring my closet for my Fall jacket.

"Where is it? Has anyone seen my Fall jacket? It isn't in my closet and I need to leave, now!"

"What's a 'Fall jacket,' Mom? Are you planning to slip on something?"

"What?"

"Well, why else would you wear a Fall jacket if you weren't planning to trip?"

"Not a 'fall,' it's a Fall-Fall jacket. Geez, I don't have time for this. Do you know where it is?"

"That clears up everything, and no, I do not know where you put your clothes. Gawd Mom, if you would just put your stuff up where it belongs, you'd be able to find it…"

Wise words, from my teenage wise-ass son.

There is a difference you know. (Not the teenager—the jackets). We all have different clothing for different reasons. Call them quirks, but mine are all about jackets and shoes.

I have my dog walking jacket, my heavy coat, my dress coat, my only-wear-out-to-fun-events-at-night jacket, my light-weight jacket, (and well, yes, I could keep going). Don't judge me, it may be an illness. In particular, I was looking for my light-weight jacket. Finally, I found it—in my closet, sandwiched and tucked in between my heavy coats.

I threw on my Fall friend and jammed my hands into the pockets, where I discovered a crinkled piece of paper. Curiosity piqued! I hoped I was pulling out a twenty dollar bill. But instead, as I glanced at & skimmed the piece of paper, it became clear it was a grocery list and I couldn't help thinking, "Huh? What the hell was I doing?"

GROCERY STORE-
hair dryer
turkey baster
5 Hershey Bars

Now is it just me, or am I the only one who finds this not only strange, but funny?

I have this super quick-witted friend, Miss Dee, who's amazingly hysterical and can find humor in a pile of poo. (She's the one you need to have with you when you need a quick comeback for a situation—cuz that girl can spew witty insults on the spot). Anyway, I had to brace myself when I saw she instantly commented on the list, (I mean I had to post it on my social media, right?):

"Was that the night I saw your husband and the children running through the streets in their underwear?"

With tears streaming down my face I began gasping for air from laughing hysterically. Just imagine my family doing that while being chased by a chocolate-eating MOMster carrying a hair dryer in one hand and a turkey baster in the other. The thought is a bit hard to shake. (For the record, that didn't really happen—to the best of my knowledge—then again, my memory may be slipping a bit!

Others thought it must've been one interesting recipe I was prepping for, (or possibly a very kinky experience—ooh, la, la), but one friend was quick to point out, "OMG, considering the source, this seems perfectly normal. You are, 'unexplainable,' and that is what makes you so unique, and awesome!

(Okay, we all know she added that last part so I wouldn't "unfriend" her).

But the funny part is I still have NO recollection of even making this list, let alone what it was for! Good grief, the wild turkeys who like to frequent our home, terrorizing our garden should be afraid—very afraid! I may give them a blow-out after basting them in a chocolate bath.

~

I AM THANKFUL...NO, REALLY, I AM! Life throws a lot of crappy blows at us sometimes, but this girl is always counting her blessings and looking for the silver linings. So I guess, like every year in November, it's time for me to catch up on my gratitude.

#1 So grateful to be blessed with so much to be thankful for—and I don't even mean the major mound of dishes in the sink, the mountains of laundry that need to be done and the hours of paying bills that's ahead of me tonight.

#2 Thankful for an incredible family who knows who I really am, and loves me despite it.

#3 Thankful for friends that fall under that same "family" category!

#4 Blessed with my dog who is excited to see me when I walk in the door. I mean, not once have I ever seen my husband wag his tail and lick my face to say, "Hello."

#5 Thankful that the same dog can't make negative comments when she walks in on me taking shower.

#6 Grateful I have a husband to love and cherish through good times and through bad. (Is it weird I listed the dog before him)?

#7 & #8 Grateful to be the Mama Bear of two amazing boys (um...sorry, I mean, "men") that I would die for in a heartbeat.

What? They do drive me crazy, but hey, you don't get to choose your family. Right?

#9 Blessed to hear the voice of my Baby Bear saying he's moving back to Northern California. YAY! I've missed him so much, so hearing that new plan was like hearing the voice of angels, (that is as long as that angelic voice doesn't start asking for money)!

I've always told my kids, "Home is where your mom is." (Though my child will tell you it's more like "Home is where the cheap rent is.")!

#10 So appreciative that our oldest son, who is away at sea, has been in contact with us while he's on the ship. It doesn't make the absence easier, but it lessens the worry (of wild-ship-parties-gone-wrong and/or him possibly falling overboard)!

#11 I am thankful for Miss D's PHENOMENAL Chili Verde recipe! Cuz that's what's for supper tonight. (Luckily, I made a ton and froze it, because we won't survive winter in this house without it)!

#12 Thankful for a warm fire, a snuggly evening with my hubby, and no "aftershocks" from the Chile Verde. (I mean, it's always more cozy to cuddle when you aren't wearing a gas mask)!

#13 So grateful for my father-in-law who loaned us his truck to haul firewood. (Now his car is all messy and not mine)! But he gets the last laugh, because we still have to split and stack that wood—and he doesn't.

#14 So, in making my world-famous French Onion soup tonight you would've thought I was more of a clown than a cook in the kitchen. Dropped the bottle cap to the balsamic vinegar into the near boiling soup. (Yep, now you know my secret ingredient). Caught the french bread croutons on fire—twice. And for the grand finale, proceeded to fill my house with so much smoke that it could have doubled for a fire academy training facility.

The blessing? It turned out great! *SLURP*

#15 Grateful for great friends who not only loaned us their log splitter, but came over and turned that chore into a party!

#16 Thankful I didn't have to go to the hospital to get stitches when I gashed open my finger. OWWW! (We're splitting wood, not splitting fingers—Oops, I guess I got confused).

#17 Thankful my husband can keep up with my crazy ideas—most days!

#18 Thankful my husband's eyeballs did NOT pop out of their sockets when I caught him eye-rolling me just because I suggested painting the ceiling today.

#19 Um...thankful that huge vein in my husband's neck didn't actually burst when I told him I wasn't too fond of the new paint color on the ceiling.

#20 So thankful that the new paint color on the ceiling is absolutely perfect! Second time's the charm.

#21 So grateful I survived not only the grocery store today, but my favorite box store, Costco, too. Somehow I managed to get through without brawling over brussel sprouts, crack-a-lackin' over cranberries, tussling over turkey, and wrestling over the last decent bottle of wine in the store. (I am still a little miffed about losing the squash skirmish—that last butternut beauty was mine, I tell ya)!

I do want to offer an public apology to the man whose foot I ran over in the store:

"I am ever so sorry sir, it was operator error. The store was out of shopping carts, so when I was forced to use the flatbed trolley to wrangle out my goods, including the 20lb bag of cat food, the 40 lb jug of cat litter, the 40lb bag of chicken feed and the 50lb bag of dog food, and I asked you to please pardon me, (so I wouldn't run over you), and you looked at me like I was out of my frickin' mind, it was bound to happen. So again, sorry it occurred, but please don't say I didn't warn you."

I can still see the look in that guy's eyes. It was like a cross between "deer in the headlights" and "Go ahead, make my day." So I did. That'll teach him about being an ass when someone is trying to help him.

#22 OHHHHHHHHH! So grateful NOT to be the lady outside Costco yesterday!!! So you know how heavy those trolley cart things are, right? Boy, once you get your momentum, it's hard to stop it. Well, I'm just getting outside the store, and this little boy keeps walking right in front of my cart—like ankle biting distance.

So I fake-cheerfully say, "Excuse me, excuse me Sweetie," thinking his mom is sane and is going to tell her kid to move out of the way before I mow him over, right? WRONG!!

Instead, she looks over and fake-smiles me back, asking, "Yes, what do you need?"

I was like WTF!!! (Which means Wednesday, Thursday, Friday, of course—I mean there is a kid present in this scenario, and I'm sure at this moment he could read my mind).

"What do I need? WHAT DO I NEED, LADY!? I need you to yank your kid's ass out of the way before I turn him into a frickin', flippin' pancake, sweetheart!!"

(Of course, I didn't say any of that, because my inner good girl was on high alert—but I did give her a stern glare that said it all. So that counts, right? Damn beyotch!)

#23 Today I am grateful that I spent three hours at the dentist office, rather than three hours at the grocery store (because, yes, I woke in the middle of the night with the HORROR that I had forgotten to buy the dinner rolls yesterday—- NOOOOO!).

Of course, it's now been three hours since I left the dental chair, after biting my dentist's finger, (not once, but twice).

HEY! Serves him right for sticking it in my mouth when I was starving for lunch.

Don't judge me. It would not have happened had they not made me wait an hour and a half to be seen. I am still numb, got chocolate drool all over my face, and according to my youngest son, I am just beginning to talk without sounding drunk. (What a peach).

Regardless, I am ever so thankful to have two old fillings replaced before I crack them on some culinary creation tomorrow!

~

THANKFUL FOR THANKSGIVING

When I reflect on some of the best holidays ever spent, many of those memories come from celebrating Thanksgiving. Hands down, the ultimate best ones of those were spent on the beaches of Mexico with friends and family; however, there were some pretty good ones stateside, as well.

The first year after a long streak of being on vacation for Thanksgiving, I was a little leery of how it would go.

I mean, I no sooner got home from the dentist, (the day before Thanksgiving), when I realized I forgot a couple of things for Thanksgiving dinner. I was clearly out of my groove.

I'm not sure what was more painful? The trip to the dentist, or what I was about to bravely do...cuz NO ONE goes to the store on Thanksgiving Eve on purpose, (unless they are there to spectate the sport of complete pandemonium while last second shoppers wrestle over the the last can of cranberry jelly)!

I wrote a note to my family, in the event I never returned:

"Dear Family I love so much,

I have made an error in gross proportions. I forgot to defrost the turkey for tomorrow. No worries though. I read online that I might be able to speed it up with blow drying it from the inside out, (but my hair dryer is on the fritz). I also need a baster for the bird. UGH!!! Wish me luck everybody—I'm goin' in! If I never return, just know I love you and that would obviously do anything for you all...even go to a grocery store on Thanksgiving Eve.

Love, Mom

PS: You all owe me BIG!!!"

(I survived the outing, thank heavens, and scarfed an entire chocolate bar in the car on the way home—What? It was for stress relief...always gotta keep a few bars on hand, just in case. Ya know?)

Anyway, as the morning dawned, I knew it would be great and that I had so much to be thankful for! I was thankful I got to sleep in, thankful for the coffee my husband served me in bed, thankful I didn't have to cook that year. (Yes, I really said that—weird, I know—but the turkey didn't thaw so I pulled out an Enchilada Casserole and roasted the turkey the next day), thankful I had my guys under the same roof. Most of all, at that moment, I was ever soooooooo thankful not to be my neighbor who lived behind us. They had the misfortune of hosting a loud, broken down garbage truck in front of their house—for several hours (starting a little before 6am). Now that REALLY STINKS!!!

Yes, was one lucky lady. We had AC/DC blasting, boys all playing pool, & cocktails being poured!!! YAY! In reality, it felt like a mini vacation in the Giacomini House to me!

(I cling to that memory, considering the following year turned out the be one of the worst Thanksgivings ever, with all the makings of a bad country song: dog died, car broke down, sick kid, bills we couldn't pay, medical crap. OMGosh! Just when I thought it couldn't get worse, it did! I remember waiting for the Silver Lining to crack me over the head any moment. That's when I took stock of my top 5 Best Thanksgivings—and those were definitely the previous five years in a row—so we had been on a great streak for awhile, so we were bound to have an off year eventually.)

Even when we were missing the beaches of Mexico our first year back stateside, we realized, who needs Mexico when you've got a day in pjs, Mexican food, Ping Pong Tournaments, Pre-Black Friday Shopping & the movies with the people you love most in the world? I am so thankful for these three guys—even if they make me cuckoo!

Heck, I even got a quick nap in before I got up at 2:30am to go shop til I dropped!!! Life was good!

In the words of my favorite Thanksgiving poem:

May your stuffing be tasty,
May your turkey be plump,
May your potatoes and gravy have never a lump.
May your yams be delicious
And your pies take the prize,
And may your Thanksgiving dinner stay off your thighs! ~Author unknown

BLACK FRIDAY—IT IS NOT FOR THE FAINT OF HEART

Have you ever noticed that everyone stops writing what they are thankful for after Thanksgiving?

It's not that people aren't thankful suddenly overnight. It's just that they are suffering from a major combination of a massive food hangover, plus the shock of hearing their scale scream, "YEOOOOOWWWW, GET OFF ME!" as they stepped on it the next day. Not to mention, they are dealing with all that leftover turkey.

I get so tired of leftover turkey, but the interesting thing is, I never get tired of wine. (Maybe since there's no such thing as leftover wine).

One thing is for sure, the day after Thanksgiving, I am praising the Lord for stretch denim, and the person who invented it! (I really gotta stay away from the truffles)! Let's be honest, have you ever walked into the bathroom first thing in the morning, turned on the light, looked in the mirror and screamed, "Aaaaacccckkkkkkkkk!"??? I'm telling you, it can make your heart skip a beat!

Last Thanksgiving, I confided in some friends, "I didn't know who the hell was looking back at me in that damn mirror!"

Addy remarked, "Girl. ummmm, HELLO, that happens to me nearly every flippin' day!"

"Well, I just had to designate our playroom (where I workout) a NO PHOTO ZONE!"

Milly was all, "What the hell?"

"Yes, because my dang kids are snapping shots while I workout, and posting them on their pages or tweets or snaps, or whatever it is the those little twits are twiddling on their phones. Damn teenagers, they think they are sooo funny."

Laughing hysterically, Milly messaged my oldest son, "I'll give you $20 to see that photo. Tee hee."

So I begin messaging my oldest son, as well, "Hmmmm...$20 or me taking away your driving privileges? Tough choice buddy, but go ahead, 'Make my day!' (I can save a bundle by cancelling your car insurance)!!!"

Yep, I went there. I pulled the biggest card I had with that kid. And I won.

It was worth it—I KNOW what I looked like in that photo, and I was actually doing this as a public service effort to save the world from being scarred for life (in the event it went viral)!

You are welcome world!

Have you also ever noticed that after Thanksgiving, people are also dealing with sleep deprivation from going Black Friday shopping all night long? I mean really, all the physical aches and pains from wrestling all the other crazies out shopping for Black Friday, it's exhausting! I know this first hand, because I used to be one of those crazies.

Nowadays, though, when Thanksgiving rolls around, I consider myself not necessarily older, but definitely wiser. To me, the day is an extension of Thanksgiving, so now it is about appreciating the little things more, and realizing that the big things are not such a big deal. For me, it's valuing time with my family, whether we're cheering at a football game or snuggled up on a couch. And it's about feeling rich with the friendships that warm our hearts every day—and reflecting on those who enriched our lives when they were with us. The day is about remembering that as long as you have your family & friends, you have all you need. It's not about plotting the sales ads and putting together a strategy on how to hit the best sales in record time. (Although back in the day, I was a master at it)!

It's about putting on spanx to hold in your newfound stuffing from the day before, not donning tackle gear to protect yourself from being crushed in the crowds. Like I said, I used to be one of those maniacs. Aahhh the memories!

I actually remember thinking that walking into a department store at 3am with the rest of my town, and standing in line for 2.5 hours was worth it. Then one year I ventured out and it took me an hours to find everything I needed. I got in line and stood there about an hour when I realized the line was still about 2 hours long and the sale was over in 60 minutes. So I did the math, and I threw in the towel (including the ones I planned to buy at 75% off). Sure, I lost an hour of my life in line, but gained two and maybe some perspective on self-worth! I realized my time is much more valuable than these Black Friday deals. Plus, it finally occurred to me that I could just buy everything online, while hanging out with my family, watching movies and catching up. Now THAT is the best bargain ever!

That was the last time I ever embarked on a Black Friday sale extravaganza. The thrill was gone, and I think that's a good thing. Because nothing says The Season of Giving more, than a full-on brawl over a bargain (*insert object of your choice here*) that you really don't need to buy anyway.

*Older Brother: "What are you giving Mom &
Dad for Christmas?"*
Younger Brother: "My Wish List."

DECEMBER

'TIS THE SEASON TO BE JOLLY
What a bunch of fa, la, la, la, la, la!

Have any of you ever TRULY lived out an entire
month of December "jolly?" I thought not!

Come to think of it, how many times in your life
have you ever felt "jolly?" I don't think I've ever
felt jolly.

Happy? Yes.
Excited? Yes.
Enthusiastic? Yes.
Euphoric? (Hell YES! I eat chocolate, need I say
more)?

So happiness-type feels, got them covered—but
"jolly" I'd be pressed to say, "Ho, ho, ho, that's a
no, no, no."

I mean, while everyone is telling you that you
should happy with the holidays and merry about

Christmas, the truth is, it is the most STRESSFUL time of the year for most of us! I liken it to visiting that "Happiest Place in the World" amusement park place, you know the one. It sounds amazing in theory, and in its own right, it is. But reality is that it is crowded with tired parents trying to keep tabs on their grouchy children whilst sternly reminding them that they have paid dearly to be at that "happy place," so they better all slap a damn smile on their face and get ecstatic STAT. (Not that I've ever experienced that before, just saying…)!

But I digress, so back to Christmas. There are just so many expectations of the Christmas Season— most unreasonable. First of all there's that feeling that you must find the perfect gift for each of your loved ones. That is a lot of pressure to put on one's self. Then there's the pressure of all the events to attend, all the excess to indulge, and depending on where you live, there's often crappy weather to endure. My list could go on and on. The point is, it's become a "Fake it 'til you Make it" time of year. So much so, when people question, "Is there's really a Santa Claus? I figure there is a much better chance of his existence, than the truth that all of us who are buried in the consumerism B.S. are gift-giving with glee.

Sometimes this time of the year is just simply full
of sneezing, hacking, yacking and coughing.
Fevers on high, and just feeling really low.
When this strikes our home, I gotta bone to pick
with Ole St. Nick:

"DAMMIT SANTA!!!! Fix your hearing aid! I
admitted, 'I know I've been naughty so I'll take
the coal'...not 'the COLD!'"

Seriously, no one has time to be sick during the
winter holidays. Right?

Occasionally we also see this truth of this not-so-
merry-season rear its ugly head. I think I heard
some years back a particular coffee establishment
took heat for putting out their Christmas cups "too
early." Not sure if I have all the facts right, but
not only did they get the riot act for that, they then
took some guff for not putting ENOUGH
"Christmasy" messaging on the cup. What the
hell? With all the politically correct crap, no one
wins anymore. For those of you who don't get
this either, let me take a stab at spelling it out for
you:

The Christmas season is about excess,
consumerism and judging others. (Surprised yet?)
So come on people, get in the spirit and yell at
someone for not putting a frickin' reindeer on their

cup! (And, by-the-way, from what I heard, those contradictory protests did not stop the vast majority of the coffee establishment's customers from lining up for their daily five-buck-a-cup). Geez, sometimes people complain just to complain...puhleeeeease!

I mean this is so ridiculously petty, and there's more to complain about than Christmas cups, people! Besides, I've got a real complaint. A couple of years ago I decided to "Go Public." That's right. For the first time in 20 years, I found myself in a brand new, but very awkward, relationship—much to my husband's chagrin. He wasn't pleased, and I don't blame him...cuz I wasn't too sure about this new relationship either, and I really needed my husband's support to make it work.

What? NO! It wasn't another man, nor kinky shenanigans—it was with a tree! Yup, a new artificial Christmas tree.

As I worked with it, I wasn't so sure it was going to work out. I am here to testify, just because something is newer, and sparklier, doesn't mean it's better.

I missed my old artificial tree—even if it took three hours to fluff it and light it. I knew every branch, and exactly how much ribbon to buy, how many ornaments to hang—and I liked how "full" it was. This new guy was a little too scrawny for my taste. At least that's what I thought—until the day we inherited Big Bertha. Oh. My. GAWD!

Big Bertha came with a house that we bought in 2017. Picture a monster faux Christmas tree 15 feet tall and 9 feet wide. PEOPLE! I had nightmares of the thing swallowing me and my entire family whole! It took three days to put it together and decorate. It was a BEYOTCH.

I actually love decorating Christmas trees, it's my thing, and I never met one I didn't like, until I met Big Bertha (aka: The Beast). I swear I started crying by the end of day two, and continued to bawl through the holiday season, until the final day of taking it down. It was miserable.

So for 2018, I went back to the 2016 tree that I kept, (thank gawd), just in case. I now love him. His name is Slim Jim, and I can decorate the hell out of him in three hours flat! It just goes to show you that sometimes you need more time for a relationship to spark, and I look forward to 20 more years with Ole Slim.

PDQ WHOOP-DE-DO

There was a time a few years back when I actually contemplated NOT putting up the tree that year.

Just. wasn't. feeling. it.

No inspiration. Dave was lagging on putting up the lights outside too. And the boys could have cared less.

What was wrong with us? This was just not the Giacomini way. For a moment we did consider compromising & making our youngest son stand in a corner on a month long Time Out and hang ornaments from his ears or somethin'. (Hmm, in hindsight we should have done that. Maybe added some lights and put him on a rotating disc?). Now THAT would have been amusing! What am I saying? It's not too late, maybe we'll do that this year?!

Sometimes the bull crap of the season keeps me from getting into the spirit. But not to worry, when that happens I engage in the good ole "faking it til I'm making it" technique. The best thing for me to do this is to actually get off my butt and get my tree-trimmin' on. Admittedly, it really is one of my few talents...and once I trim the tree the season fills with glee. I think it's the glitter, because glitter lasts forever and how can you look drab and unspirited coated in glitter? Right?

Each year I try to decorate our tree with a different theme. It's fun, but sometimes daunting at the same time. I've decorated: cowboy trees, snowball trees, around the world trees, peppermint trees, & whimsical trees. I mean you name it, and I've probably done it.

One year, many moons ago, we decided to decorate a truly old-fashioned tree, completed with strung popcorn and gingerbread men. When it was done, it was absolutely adorable, if I do say so myself.

We were very proud of that tree, and it took days and days to prep everything to adorn it as such. After the final touches had been made decorating the tree, I remember being in another room, when I began to hear the most perplexing sound.

   "Plop. Plop. Plop, plop-plop!"

I couldn't figure out where the noise was coming from, but each "plop" sounded like it was hitting...paper??? It was soooo strange!

As I investigated, I finally found myself in the room with our freshly ornamented tree. That's when I heard it again.

Awwww, crap! It was coming from the tree.

I apprehensively moved in closer, expecting to have something spring out of the tree at any moment. "Oh shit. Oh shit. Oh shit!" I was so sure it was a rat or a squirrel or gawd-only-knows-what. As I BRAVELY crept closer, I began to discover the absolute horror.

"OH MY GAWD, OH MY GAWD, OH MY GAWD!" I screamed to my husband, (who was actually just outside putting up Christmas lights). Maybe it was my oddly weird pitchy moans of dismay that made him realize I wasn't messing around, because he rushed inside to come to come to my rescue. As he sidled up to me, it was obvious. I was in shock.

"What happened? What happened, what's going on?" he questioned urgently.

Stammering, I replied, "I, I...I heard the noise, the plopping."

"Ok, so what does that mean? What do you mean 'plopping'?"

I then numbly lifted my arm and pointed at the tree. "THEY'RE DECAPITATED!!!'

That's when he saw, for the first time, my horror. All our gingerbread men were bodiless!!!

All the time baking them. All the time threading the ribbons through their heads. All the time painstakingly decorating them. ALL GONE! All that time wasted! Down the drain.

I could tell he was stifling his laughter, but gave me a little pat on the shoulder and remarked as solemnly as possible, "That stinks! Guess we'll have to eat them now. Do we have milk?"

As I came back to my senses, he shuffled off to finish the lights, and I noticed our two big ole golden retrievers were eager to come inside. So I sadly sauntered over to the glass slider door to open it for them. I no sooner had the door opened a few inches before they both barreled inside, pushing me aside and bee-lined to the tree! They attacked the tree, knocked it over and began eating it!

"OH MY F-ING GAWD!" In fits of complete hysteria, I lunged to struggle with them both attempting to wrangle them off the tree, and throwing their hairy butts back outside.

My beautiful tree was now a big disaster.

Slowly I gathered my wits, propped the tree back up. Salvaged a bit of the strung popcorn. Then I found a couple headless gingerbread men laid on the smashed presents below. Carefully, I picked them up, blew off the pine needles and dog hair, and contemplated a little frosting surgery to reattach.

As I slunk down and sat cross-legged on the floor while trying to figure out the impending surgical procedure, a wave of emotion swept over me and I suddenly decided, "Screw it!" and devoured every bit of those little gingersnaps.

Just a case of tasty tree-trimming gone bad.

~

NAUGHTY OR NICE LIST

So here's the deal: I'm gettin' nothing for Christmas, 'cuz I've been a bad, bad girl—and I'm okay with that! My theory: Be good for 365 days to have one great night OR be bad for 365 days and have 365 great nights??? Hmmmmm...tough decision!!! *wink, wink*

It's going to be hard work to get on THAT list, since I am such an angel—but I am working on it, and taking steps toward my goal. Check out this little diddy I threw together to celebrate my newfound "badness" on my favorite social media platform:

"And what to my wondering eyes should appear, but Dave's Chocolate Chip cookies...
so I better finish my beer."

(Okay, I was really drinking a glass of wine, but it didn't rhyme. So I took creative license to alter the truth slightly. Get over it)!

In continuance of making some bad choices, my friends began to inquire on my progress:

"Hey OMG. are those lumps of coal we see in your stockings?"

I gulped hard and replied, "No! Just the long lasting effect from eating Dave's chocolate chip cookies." (Hmmm...maybe I should rethink my bad girl thoughts)!

"Being a BAD Girl isn't always a bad thing, ask your husband," remarked one of my smartass friends.

"Not so sure about that, but I do believe I finally made the Naughty List this year. I kinda did something bad. Real bad!"

"Like the kind of bad where you're going to get a little 'sexy pink bag' gift from your hubby for Christmas?"

"No, the kinda bad where I sort of just snuck into my Christmas gift and play with it. But I plan to put it back before he gets home. He'll never know—unless my son rats me out!"

"You are soooo bad!"

"WHAT? You all know patience isn't one of my virtues!!! In my defense, it was Baby Bear's idea—so I just went with it, and it was fun!!! OH CRAP! I just realized—he didn't get that gift for me, he picked up that video game for his office Christmas Party gift exchange. Oops! Guess I'll just have to keep it now...oh darn. The sacrifices I make for this family."

~

WAND-ERFUL WISH LIST

So even though I feel I've lobbied a logical case for being naughty year-round, it's going to take some practice. I've decided, just in case I'm back on the Nice List again, I'm making out my Wish List:

1. A full night's rest
2. A Magic Wand

Yep. that's it. If bestowed upon me, I promise to use my powers for good, not evil.

What? You think that's weird about good vs. evil powers for sleep? If you do, then you haven't seen the power of energy that emanates from a hard working mother of two teenage sons, once she's had a great night's sleep. Tellin' ya, on the rare occasion it happens, I'm like a whole different woman!

That said, I set to work writing a letter to Santa:

"Dear Santa:

While I think I may have finally made the Naughty List this year, I've also been undeniably good too. I drag my a$$ out of bed every day to exercise (& do my FB while riding my exercise bike). I don't drink (every night). And, I'm kind to small kids (well, most days). It's not my fault others don't get along with me...I try! So, as you can see Santa, I deserve a few things that I really need: 1. Sleep (a full night here and there would be a bonus) 2. A Magic Wand and 3. A new pair of stiletto cowboy boots. They are very

sexy…(oops), I mean, cute & practical! Thanks!
♥

LOVE YOU SANTA,
Miss OMG"

I thought that should do the trick so I mailed the letter and then I decided to post on social media—figuring somehow that may help my dreams come true! (Especially if certain friends were to share my list with a certain awesome Santa—hint, hint).

Problem was, the next day we discovered that a certain cherub of ours royally screwed up and left the stove on for 12 hours. We were suddenly anticipating a $500 propane bill. So I sent an overnight letter immediately. Yep, begged Santa to ditch my list and pay my propane bill instead. (The kind ole chap brought me the sexy cowboy boots anyway! Guess my Santa is a little partial to girls on the Naughty List after all)!

~

TO SHOP OR TO DROP? THAT IS THE QUESTION

Whether it's shopping the stores or dropping cookie dough for eight million dozen Christmas Cookies, it is a very busy and very exhausting time of year. But I've learned to survive the season with a few shortcuts:

1. I don't make dinner on the days I bake Christmas Cookies—I figure the kids can just lick the bowl! So bite my big, fat brownie—cuz dessert, it's the "new dinner."

2. When making my famous truffles, I multi-flask that task and combine it with Happy Hour—that way my truffles get a little bit of the good stuff in them—and I get a little of the good stuff in me! WIN-WIN! However, when ya'll hear the giant sonic boom—it's my butt expanding from eating too many Hot Cinnamon Liqueur Truffles!!!!

3. Switching gears to shopping. I send the husband out for last minute errands while I go into covert, mass gift wrapping execution! You've never seen such great teamwork when we divide and conquer!

4. Send the teens to pick up the gift of my husband's dreams, is another one of my favorite tips.   While I am busy running other errands, I send the boys to pick up the latest cool thing-a-ma-bobber. I figure it's one of those new-fangled thing-a-ma-jigs I could care LESS about, and the

boys know everything about. They have fun shopping and I get to check one more thing off my list. Guys and their gadgets, good grief!!!

5. Racing heart, breathless, butterflies...trembling all over...only one thing truly makes me feel this way: SHOPPING! And I do NOT mean this in a good way.

The biggest reason why: PARKING PANDEMONIUM PANIC-ATTACKS! So I keep in mind, when it comes to Christmas Shopping it is important to be safe, proceed with caution, and if anyone steals your parking spot, try not to go all raging-rabid-turd-ogre on'em! It is the holiday season of love, right? I had to learn this the hard way:

"Dear Lady in the Big Ass SUV who stole my parking spot,

I could rant & rave at you, since I obviously had my blinker on, & waited patiently for those people to pack & leave (long before you showed up and swooped in), but I'm sure your head's too far up your a$$ to hear me out. Instead, just want to say that your license plate that reads, 'IMABTCH' suits you.

Merry Christmas."

OMGosh!!! I knew she knew she stole it from me too, because she wouldn't look at me as I continued to sit there with my jaw on the ground, watching her get out of her car—trying to keep myself from going all crazy-ass-monster-truck-rally on her!!! (Let's be rational here, my little commuter car vs. her giant tank SUV? I'm not delusional. Besides, I'm new to the Naughty List and my license plate still reads "NCEGRL1").

6. When Christmas Shopping is done, it's DONE!! There is no way in H-E-L-L I'm going back out there again—not unless I'm packing some serious heat (aka: Xanax and a couple Martinis under my belt)! Remember, people are rude, crazed and flat out idiots. As previously noted, the parking lots are beacons to some of the longest traffic jams I've seen in ages. And the crowds are an anxiety attack waiting to happen! Instead, it's better to enjoy a quiet evening by the fire, enjoying the peace and serenity with family. (Who am I kiddin'? Peace and serenity here? In my house? HA! Got Valium???)

7. One thought from a friend on the ease of Christmas Shopping is to drive to the bank & simply withdraw money. Then proceed to nearest convenience store and buy a pack of Christmas

cards. Go home, open a bottle of wine and write a nice note in each card, add the money.

VOILA! Done & done.

8. Another friend advises to shop at 9pm on weeknights. You'll get front row parking and the stores are practically empty. (I agree, this would be a phenomenal idea, if I wasn't already passed out on the couch from wrapping too many of those Christmas Card-Money-Gift-Letter-with-Wine thingys)!

9. My friend Addy likes to remind us that she skips over all the stress of the Christmas season EVERY year—She's Jewish.

10. IT'S A WRAP! Instead of several wrapping sessions where you lug out the wrapping supplies and put them back, do what I do: Get up at 5:30am on Christmas Eve to wrap gifts non-stop while hiding in your closet. Now keep in mind, it took me over 5 hours to wrap everything that will take under 5 minutes to open.

(Hmmm...in reflection, something just doesn't seem right with this process, right)???

There really is no other feeling than that moment when you realize you are done, done & done with

Christmas Shopping! It's a bit of euphoria mixed with dismay of being finished—of course, that's because I now have the credit card bills to prove it!!!

~

T'WAS THE NIGHT BEFORE CHRISTMAS
They say that when you're stressed, a great thing to do is journal your feelings. Funny thing is, you know when "they" say "they say," we rarely know who "they" is who is saying such stuff. Right?

Just saying.

Needless to say, I decided I needed to take a moment on Christmas Eve from the insanity of the season and pour out my thoughts, (and yes, when I say "pour" I do mean "pour," as in wine—lots and lots of wine)!

T'was the day before Christmas, and in the kitchen of the house,
a creature was stirring, it was Mickie (not the mouse).

The stockpot heated and veggies chopped up with care,
in hopes that a savory soup soon would be there.

The children were nestled all snug in their beds,
because they're still teenagers and too lazy to
even lift up their heads.

And Mama Mickie (aka: MissOMG) so busy
making Salsa Rustica from scratch,
had just seared the meat and was longing for a
nap.

She did not move quietly, in fact she made such a
clatter,
and the fresh sautéed herbs wafted up from the
platter.

to melt up some sage butter to pour over the sweet
potatoes she mashed,
Away to the fridge she flew like a flash.

and her hubby tasted and tested, while she
simmered sauce down on low,
But knew to she'd have to transform into a
culinary hero, Super Mick.

The sun at noon gave the room a happy glow,
And she was thrilled, cuz the soup was now done.

but forgotten items she feared,
then remembered that Dave bought a keg full of
beer.

*More rapid than boiling broth, her courses they
came,
and she whistled and shouted and called them by
name:*

*"Now Tuscan Soup! Now Maple Sage Butter!
Now, sweet potatoes, now mimosas!*

*On, truffles, On Hot Damn!!
On, pasta sauce & parmesana romana!*

*To the Sherry Cake!
To the salad!
Now appetizers! Dessert!
Cocktails, cocktails, cocktails for all!"*

*As dry leaves of thyme turned into a prime rib
rub,
when they meet with rosemary, and a tub*

*of oranges so sweet and juicy, fresh squeezed,
and for the marinade you need to add Jack
Daniels, indeed!*

*And then, in a sprinkling, she ran to the cake,
and powder sugared it till it looked like
snow...that was fake.*

*As she drew in smell of the spices so strong,
She could help but think of past Christmases of
long.*

The chocolate was too thick for the truffles, tisk tisk,
so she thinned out the lumps with cream and a whisk .

But thinning out chocolate will not make you skinny.
The thought of it made her laugh at the irony,

Her eyes—how they twinkled! Her dimples, how merry!
She set the table with roses, and dropped in her drink a big cherry!

Her husband wrapped presents, complete with a bow,
and the thought of a storm would be great if it snowed.

The poppy seeds from a breakfast bagel were stuck in her teeth,
and the baked bread she dreamed of was shaped like a wreath.

She couldn't taste everything or she'd get a little round belly,
but her gluten-free pancake would sure taste better with jelly.

To make all these dishes, she could've used the help of an elf,
but when she finished she laughed and was proud of herself.

Another cup of coffee? No the caffeine she would dread,
but to catch a wink of sleep, would mean going off to bed.

She spoke not a word, as she remembered more work,
and her oldest son helped her set the table...she didn't raise a jerk.

And laying down on the couch while blowing his nose,
The youngest made a few attempts to help, cuz that's how it goes.

Knowing dinner was ready, she wanted to whistle,
Because Mickie knew tomorrow sleeping in she'd be able.

So off to celebrate, with the stove out of sight,
"Happy Christmas to all, and to all a good night!"

I'm starting to understand why I gain so much weight during the winter holidays. It's the journaling, for sure!

YOU KNOW IT'S CHRISTMAS W/TEENS WHEN...

When there comes a time that the night before Christmas a mandatory sleep-IN time is designated & the kids complain it's still TOO early, you know you are celebrating Christmas with teenagers. Presents haven't been opened first thing on Christmas morning because the kids would rather eat, text & watch slapstick comedies on tv, then sleep some more, rather than do anything else.

HOWEVER!

In our family, we have a tradition of whoever finds the green pickle ornament on the tree first gets to open the first gift. Have I ever mentioned my family is very competitive? Yep, sometimes the poor tree takes a beating...(and I swear it's why our 20 year old tree had to retire).

That said, you know it's Christmas with teens when they're searching for the green pickle on the tree & their mom is posting on FB with it hidden in her robe pocket!

I like to refer to it as Yuletide Payback! Good times, good times!

Here's the deal though. When this special day is all said and done, I'm able to reflect and realize I got some great gifts for Christmas: A house full of family, some quiet time laughing over Christmas movie classics with my boys, and a very unexpected "Thank you for everything, momma," as I walk upstairs to go to bed first. (Guess which one of those was my favorite gift of all)? Yep, Christmas with teen-agers—wouldn't trade these moments for the world!

~

YULETIDE YIN YANG

REALITY CHECK: OMGosh! It was the day after Christmas, not too long ago, when I realized I'm officially old.

A week before the holiday, I actually paid FULL PRICE for an ice cream cake for the convenience, instead of painstakingly making one. WTFrick?

Then on that particular December 26th, (my favorite day of the year), I decided sleep was more important than saving 50% on holiday crap for next year.

I remember waking up thinking, "WHAT IS HAPPENING TO ME???"

As reality set in, I realized I'd lost my shopping mojo. As I pondered whether I should get out of bed and revive it, (or not!). I decided I could easily compromise. So I went downstairs, poured myself a cup o' decaf, and headed back up to bed with my laptop to cyber shop. Half hour later, my coffee was finished and so was I—finished with shopping 'til I drop, for good. Why? (Because I discovered the best cure for impulse buying: check out my current credit card balance before I even dare open a favorite shopping website).

~

'TIS THE SEASON TO WORKOUT
WOW! The day after Christmas I seem to find muscles I never ever knew I had before (or at least forgot I had)!!! No wonder those little Italian grammas never get fat! Rolling out raviolis is hard work—and my arms feel like they're going to fall off! Why did we start this tradition? Owwweeeee! I think I pulled a pec! (But it was worth it)! Dinner for about 25. Yup, that's why I don't go snowboarding with the kids on this glorious day off. I figured one pull up, and I'd

lose my right arm! (Plus the idea of a quiet house all to myself, now that it a great gift to ME)!

Oh, but my dearest husband is so sweet, right before he left for a day on the slopes, while I was still under the warm, cozy covers, he gave me a little something to show he does love me! That's right, he had a hot cinnamon mocha waiting for me on my nightstand. YUMMM! And CRAP! That means I need to actually workout now...(but it was worth every sip)!

~

POST TRAUMATIC HOLIDAY STRESS DISORDER

Okay, in comparison to the build-up of the holiday season, I totally consider December 25th to be my "Lazy Day." Seriously, it only takes another day before I am straight up BORED! There's nothing to do—oh gawd, all this extra time on my hands. No shopping, no cooking, no making the house appear clean when it really isn't, no nothing...nothing, nothing, nothing! Oh, except to relax. Guess I could try something new and learn how to do that???

However, those who know me, know that I happen to be relaxation-challenged. Like to unwind, I like to make lists, and sometimes I make lists about the lists. I also like to clean out my closet and purge the crap out of everything. But I only do this when I have a spare day—which is a rarity—so I'm really not as warped as you think. Another thing that happens when I have a bit of downtime is come up with new projects—lots and lots of new projects for everyone! So in my house, it's really to everyone's benefit, (and our wedded bliss), to keep me very busy with my own endeavors.

One year, I felt really punched in the gut. We waltzed through the holidays-no problem. Then we battled the traffic all day getting home from vacation in Southern California, to our home about 45 minutes north of Sacramento—which was worse than braving the crowds at The Happiest Place on Earth (our Christmas gift to our boys that year). Suddenly, the major momentum of the holiday merriment skidded to halt! Holidays over. Mini-Vacation over. Then the oldest kid jumped into his car 15 minutes after we pulled up, and he left to go back to college. I HATE THAT MOMENT EVERY SINGLE TIME!!! Suddenly a tidal wave of emptiness, boredom and loneliness washed over me. UH OH!!! We all know what that leads to!!!

"HEY HONEY!!! WE NEED A NEW PROJECT!"

I've noticed that one of my personal projects I get busy doing is amping up the exercise after the holidays. Like many of my friends, I begin praising the elastic god the day after the winter holidays end. And when that elastic is starting to pinch off my circulation, trust me, that's when it's obvious there is such a thing as too much Christmas cheer. It's time to hit the treadmill ASAP.

So it's back to a healthy lifestyle again, and my dogs are thrilled about that too (cuz you know what they say, "If your dog is fat, YOU need more exercise"). But that can all happen right after our lunchtime sangrias.

HEY! Don't judge me, it's Winter Break! PLUS, a sangria makes cleaning house so much more fun. (Okay, that's a big ass lie. I really need at least two or three for that to be fun)! WHAT? Do you know how much crap I have shoved into closets to achieve that "my house is super clean all the time" look? Believe me, you DO NOT want to know—and for your own safety, never open a closet door when visiting my house!

So, while I sipped some sangria this particular day after Christmas, I pondered my productivity, or lack thereof, decided it was time to put pen to paper and write Santa a special thank you note, with all this leisure time on my hands:

"December 26th

Dear Santa,
Just a little note to thank you for all you brought me this year. I have to say, at first glance, it appeared that I must've been high on the Nice List for once (but now I'm starting to wonder)!? You brought me some really great presents. But then I got to thinking that was just a ruse, because when I woke up today, I saw what else you left. Well mister, thanks, but no thanks. I think you need to come back, because I have a few things I want to return.

First of all, I have a whole lot of wrapping paper that I want to send back. Yes, granted it's used—all rumpled and crumpled and all over my house—plus mangled bows to match. But, could you please do that little finger on the side of your nose thing, and up the chimney all of it will go? Much appreciated.
Secondly, what the h-e-double-hockey-sticks did you do to my kitchen??? What was once a pristine place that looked like no one ever used it,

is now a pile of dishes and pots and pans and gawd-only-knows-what. Santa, seriously. I'm a minimalist, I really do not need all of that. Please dash away, dash away, dash away all of it.

And last, but not least, you left me a couple extra pounds on my scale today, Ole St. Nick. Now I do not want to sound ungrateful, dear sir, but these I can certainly do without. In fact, if you would expedite a speedy removal, I'd be ever so indebted.

Thank you again for all your generosity!

Love and warmest winter wishes,
Olivia Michele Giacomini

PS: What's with all the glitter everywhere? Really? What kind of Christmas magic are you working around here, big guy??? Good grief! Talk about overkill!!!"

It was not long before I received a reply. At first, I figured it may be a form letter addressing my concerns, but the more I read, it was obvious that the letter was written by the jolly man in red, himself:
"Dear Miss Olivia Michele,

Last night on my rounds, I flew by once or twice,

(In YOUR house I gotta double-check who's being naughty or nice)!

But I found people laughing and smiling and heard some screams of exclaim,
While you all played a cut-throat Guess-What-I'm-Drawing-type game.

I had been by earlier, to see what I adore,
You all had opened gifts & they were strewn all over the floor.

Of course that was after the feast your had goin',
The food never stopped and the wine was a-flowin'.

But not one complaint, did ever I hear…
So off I went on my trip with my tiny reindeer.

Missy, I understand the gifts I gave overwhelmed you,
But I say grab a mop, and broom and a vacuum.

And with every dish you wash and mess you swipe,
Remember the friends & family you have in your life.

You are blessed, yes so blessed, to have over all who came,

*And you need to feel grateful, because that mess is
no shame!*

*I left it for you to remember so dear,
All the fun and the laughter YOU had right there.*

*Love and kisses from the North Pole,
Santa"*

WHOA!

Talk about laying on the guilt! Goodness sakes
alive, Santa must be taking lessons from my
mother. I realized quickly I better smooth things
over with ole Santa:

"Dear Santa,

*Thank you for the mess you gave me. It was very
thoughtful of you. It took me hours and hours and
hours to clean. But you were right, it brought me
a huge smile remembering the special day I was
lucky to have with my friends and family. (And
winning that Pictionary game was just icing on
the cake)!*

So thank you again for thinking of me.

Lotsa love,
OMG"

I figured that would be the end of it. But ole Kris Kringle had to have the last word:

"Dear Miss OMG,
I am so glad you enjoyed your gifts with glee,
Now, I have one thing I might mention…kind-of a
sore spot with me.

Next time I visit, please don't leave out
Low-cal cookies and fizzy water, it just makes me
pout.

'Til next year, be a good girl,
Santa (aka: The Big Guy)

PS: I will never understand how those boys of
yours got "elf" from that drawing they made???
(They will need to work hard to get off the
Naughty List for next year for sure)!"

GOOD-BYE & GOOD RIDDANCE

Well, it's that time again, when everyone starts bashing the current year and praying for a better one. But, what about the good things that happened to all of us? (Easy to forget sometimes). I was sharing my humble opinion with good friends yesterday that I believe it's all about what you choose to focus on. I choose to focus on the positive. My goals for next year are to surround myself with positive people and participate more in random acts of kindness. I'll deal with the negative things, but I will appreciate each of life's blessings that come my way. I plan to enjoy my friends and family—and if all else fails, I will runaway with my boyfriend, Capt. Morgan, and never look back!

(My friends were quick to point out that I probably didn't realize that my boyfriend was also dating all of them...hmmm. That's okay, since I figured that was nothing compared to my friend whose biggest blessing of the year was potty training—so there's that).

But before we close out the year, I just want to mention one last thing to all you parents out there. Wouldn't you all agree, that the best blessing to start off each new year is when you hear that beautiful, sweet sound on New Year's Eve, of the garage door opening and your kids walking in the door, safe & sound? Can't speak for you, but as for myself, now this mom can sleep.

Happy New Year all! And may your whole year, every year, bring you many moments of joy and laughter!

ABOUT THE AUTHOR

Specializing in social commentary, Miss OMG devours every opportunity to express her love for food, wine and travel though hilarious anecdotes by day, and is a Chicken farmer by night. Between being the mother of two crazy young men, while married to the yin to her yang, and working as an elementary school teacher & principal for many almost twenty years, Miss OMG has experienced more hysterical life episodes that she'll ever be able to write about. But she's determined to try!

You can find this forever Foodie/Winer writing about her latest adventures in DayTripperMag.com and on her Facebook page.

Follow her today at:
https://www.facebook.com/OMGMissOMG/

or

https://www.facebook.com/DayTripperMag/

Be sure to look for Miss OMG's next book,
Expected to release in Fall/Winter of 2019

www.ingramcontent.com/pod-product-compliance
Lightning Source LLC
Chambersburg PA
CBHW060930040426
42445CB00011B/867